READING
for Academic Purposes

Introduction to EAP

Robyn Brinks Lockwood

Stanford University

Kelly Sippell

Series Editor: Keith S. Folse

University of Michigan Press
Ann Arbor

ISBN-13: 978-0-472-03669-1

2019   2018   2017   2016   4   3   2   1

Acknowledgments

Robyn would like to thank Keith Folse, series editor, for his feedback and input, and her co-author, Kelly Sippell, for sharing her vast knowledge and time to make this a valuable textbook. This series benefits from their expertise. Personal thanks to her family, parents, June and Virgil, and husband, John, for their unwavering support as she worked through dinners and vacations. Special thanks to Drs. Virgil Albertini and David Slater (and other former professors) who gave her a love for literature and language that are especially evident in this series of books.

The publisher, series editor, and authors would like to thank the educational professionals whose reviews helped shape the *Four Point* series and saw earlier versions of this material, particularly those from these institutions:

Auburn University
Boston University CELOP
Central Piedmont Community College
Colorado State University
Daytona Beach Community College
Duke University
Durham Technical College
Georgia State University
Harding University
Hillsborough Community College
Northern Virginia Community College, Alexandria Campus
Oregon State University
University of California, San Diego
University of Nevada at Las Vegas
University of North Carolina, Charlotte
Valencia Community College
Virginia Commonwealth University

Grateful acknowledgment is made to the following authors, publishers, and individuals for permission to reprint copyrighted or previously published materials.

Encyclopaedia Brittanica for two entries in *The Ideas that Changed the World*. Copyright © 2010 by Encyclopaedia Britannica, Inc. Used with permission.

The Free Press, a Division of Simon & Schuster, Inc., from GREAT PROJECTS by James Tobin. Copyright © 2001 by Great Projects Film Co. All rights reserved. Used with permission.

Harper Collins for *In Our Defense: The Bill of Rights in Action* by Ellen Alderman and Caroline B. Kennedy. Copyright © 1991 by Ellen Alderman and Caroline B. Kennedy. Used with permission.

Harper Collins for excerpts from *The Gardner Heist: The True Story of the World's Largest Unsolved Art Theft* by Ulrich Boser. Copyright © 2009. Used with permission.

Oxford University Press for *Word Myths: Debunking Linguistic Urban Myths* by David Wilton. Copyright © 2004. Used with permission.

Simon and Schuster for the critical introduction to *The Good Earth* by Pearl S. Buck. Copyright © 2005.

Gordon Tapper for his introduction and notes to *My Ántonia* by Willa Cather, Barnes & Noble Classic. Copyright © 2003. Used with permission.

The University of Michigan Museum of Art for *The Break-Up of the Ice (La Débâcle or Les Glaçons)*, 1880, acquired through the generosity of Russell B. Stearns (LS&A, 1916) and his wife, Andrée B. Stearns, of Dedham, Massachusetts (1976/2.134). Used with permission.

The University of Michigan Museum of Art for material from *Monet at Vétheuil: The Turning Point* by Annette Dixon, Carole McNamara, and Charles Stuckey. Copyright © 1998. The Regents of the University of Michigan.

The University of Michigan Press for *Topics in Language and Culture* by Steven Brown and Jodi Eisterhold. Copyright © 2004. Used with permission.

Every effort has been made to contact the copyright holders for permission to reprint borrowed material. We regret oversights that may have occurred and will rectify them on future printings of this book.

4 Point Overview

The **4 Point** series is designed for English language learners whose primary goal is to succeed in an academic setting. While grammar points and learning strategies are certainly important, academic English learners need skills-based books that focus on reading, listening, and speaking, as well as the two primary language bases of vocabulary and grammar.

The Introduction to EAP level is designed for students in academic programs who need a more general introduction to authentic academic content. The discrete skills **4 Point** volumes are designed for programs and courses that want a more intensive focus on authentic academic content in one skill area. We have created these volumes on individual skills because customers wanted authentic academic content at this level, but they wanted to be able to focus on one skill at a time. The ultimate goal is to help your students improve these skills and earn a 4.0 (G.P.A.).

4 Point covers academic skills while providing reinforcement and systematic recycling of key vocabulary and further exposure to grammar issues. The goal of this series is to help students improve their ability in each of these critical skills and thereby enable the students to have sufficient English to succeed in their final academic setting, whether it be community college, college, or university.

Many ESL students report great difficulties upon entering their academic courses after they leave the safe haven of their English class with other non-native speakers and their sympathetic and caring ESL teachers. Their academic instructors speak quickly, give long reading assignments due the next day, and deliver classroom lectures and interactions at rapid, native speed. In sum, ESL students who have gone through a sheltered classroom setting are in for a rather rude awakening in a new learning situation where English is taken for granted and no one seems to understand the new reality of the dilemmas facing ESL students. Through these materials, we hope to lessen the shock of such an awakening. The activities in **4 Point** achieve the goal of helping students experience what life beyond the ESL classroom is like while they are still in our sheltered classrooms.

These volumes focus very heavily on vocabulary because language learners know that they are far behind their native-speaker counterparts when it comes to vocabulary. Each book highlights key vocabulary items, including individual words, compound words, phrasal verbs, short phrases, idioms, metaphors, collocations, and longer set lexical phrases. In learning vocabulary, the two most important features are frequency of retrievals (i.e., in exercises) and the spacing between these retrievals. Interactive web-based exercises provide additional opportunities for students to practice their academic vocabulary learning at their convenience (www.press.umich.edu/elt/compsite/4Point/).

Using the Exercises in This Book (Reading)

Each unit includes two reading passages on the same topic within a field of academic study. The exercises accompanying the readings are meant to strengthen a range of reading skills, notably:

- understanding the big picture
- developing vocabulary acquisition strategies
- developing strategies for understanding academic texts through before-reading, during-reading, and after-reading strategies
- summarizing, as it relates to reading

Special attention was given to providing material that would expose students to the types of texts that might be common in difficult academic disciplines. **The goal is to provide students with a variety of strategies/tools to master whatever academic texts they may encounter. In addition, the inclusion of three types of reading strategies—before, during, and after—is unprecedented in ESL textbooks but is grounded in the realities of today's academic content and in the research on the strategies used by successful readers.**

Getting Started

The discussion questions before each reading passage should prompt students to begin thinking about relevant topics and issues. These discussions should be allowed to range freely. Often these questions provide opportunities for students to anticipate content and, therefore, may be revisited throughout the unit.

Strategy/Skill Boxes

Other types of strategies and skills—primarily related to reading and vocabulary—are highlighted at various points throughout the units. Each appears in a display box with a short explanation and is followed by an activity to explicitly practice what has been learned.

Reading for the Big Picture

Each reading in a unit is followed by short "big picture" questions. These questions are designed only to gauge student comprehension of the reading's main points.

Summarizing What You Have Read

Every reading is accompanied by an exercise in which students produce a few focused summaries. These represent only the "core" of meaning in the originals. As in any summary, students have to recognize and produce alternate wording for the concepts in the original sentence. In a focused summary, however, students also have to distinguish the sentence's central proposition(s) from the "distractions" of extra modifiers, parenthetical asides, lists of examples, and so on.

Emphasis on Vocabulary Learning

One of the best features of this book that separates it from other academic preparation books is the heavy focus on vocabulary. We recognize—as our students certainly do—that they face serious difficulties because of their limited vocabulary. The vocabulary levels of the best ESL students are often insufficient to cope with daily academic work, whether it be the vocabulary in a professor's lecture, the course book, a group discussion project, or a term paper. We would even go so far as to say that the single most important assistance we can give our students is to help them increase their academic vocabulary.

To meet this important lexical goal, this book explicitly teaches and practices a great deal of key vocabulary. Most notably, the readings are authentic and have not been watered down. In other words, they have not been rewritten in the traditional ESL-ese language.

Each unit contains two **Vocabulary Power** activities, each of which consists of eight vocabulary items in bold that students must match with the correct definitions. The vocabulary is used in context, so this activity practices vocabulary items in their natural context. This activity previews the vocabulary as well as the reading. This natural context is more difficult than the usual watered down material found in many ESL textbooks.

Learners are given a list of ten vocabulary items from the readings in **Your Active Vocabulary in the Real World**. Learners are asked to decide whether a given word is more useful in their reading, writing, listening, or speaking. In this critical-thinking task, learners are expected to consider how they might actually need this new vocabulary item. We know vocabulary is important, but we cannot teach our learners all the words they need. Therefore, **a major goal of this book is to help train our learners to become active vocabulary seekers**, which means when they encounter a new word, they need to decide if the word is one they really need to know to be able to use it in their writing or speaking or if they are more likely to hear that word in a lecture or conversation or read it in a passage. In other words, we want our learners to recognize the difference between words they need to be able to use and words they need to be able to recognize. These activities are designed to generate class discussion.

Rapid Vocabulary Review reviews the target vocabulary in the unit. It is divided into two sections—synonyms and combinations and associations. The first is straightforward: One item out of three is closest in meaning to the target item, and students indicate which one it is. The second section involves more lateral thinking. The correct answer may stand in any of several relationships to the target term. It may complete a phrase involving the target item, it may name a category to which the target item belongs, or it may state an effect of which the target item is a cause. Some students may be unfamiliar with such a non-linear form of vocabulary review, but it is an essential part of comprehensive vocabulary study. Students should be encouraged to persevere.

Crucial to the vocabulary acquisition process is the initial noticing of unknown vocabulary. Students must notice the vocabulary in some way, and this noticing then triggers awareness of the item and draws the attention of learners to the word in all subsequent encounters, whether the word is read in a passage or heard in a conversation or lecture. To facilitate noticing and then multiple retrievals of new vocabulary, we have included a chart listing approximately 20 to 25 key vocabulary items at the end of each unit. This **Vocabulary Log** has three columns and requires students to provide a definition or translation in the second column and then an original example or note about usage in the third column. In this third column, students can use the word in a phrase or sentence, or they can also add usage information about the word such as *usually negative, very formal sounding,* or *used only with the word* launch, for example. As demonstrated in *Vocabulary Myths* (Folse, 2004, University of Michigan Press), there is no research showing that a definition is better than a translation or vice-versa, so we suggest that you let students decide which one they prefer. After all, this log is each student's individual vocabulary notebook, so students should use whatever information is helpful and that will help the student remember and use the vocabulary item. If the log information is not deemed useful, the learner will not review this material—which defeats the whole purpose of keeping the notebook.

EAP Projects (Synthesizing)

Students are often expected to proceed from what they learned via reading passages. The series includes projects designed to mimic actual assignments or test questions students are likely to encounter in their academic courses. One or two prompts are for pieces that could be done in a one-hour class period or part of a class period. Typically, these prompts encourage students to do some planning as homework before the activity. There are two prompts per unit that require more outside reading and a longer finished product. They are meant to be assigned as homework and are ideal for a flipped or blended learning environment. For additional ideas about flipping using **4 Point,** see *Flip It! Strategies for the ESL Classroom* (Lockwood, 2014, University of Michigan Press). The directions in such prompts ask students to do some light research. The suggested lengths are just that—suggestions.

These long assignments are not meant to be formal. This book does not comprehensively address specific issues of formal academic writing. Teachers are free, of course, to turn one or two of these projects into something longer, more formal, and with higher stakes, if they would like to combine reading and writing. These projects are included as an appendix, so teachers are free to skip these longer projects without sacrificing learning objectives if time is short.

Contents

1

Marketing: Vision and Values

Businesses can adapt their marketing strategies depending on the products they are selling. However, some things about a business don't change, no matter what products or services the company offers. For example, the business vision, mission statement, and core values/purpose remain fairly steady. These are important because customers see them and relate them to everything the company offers. If employees know, understand, and believe in the mission and values, they are better able to help the company succeed.

Part 1: Mission Statements

Getting Started

Mission statements express a company's primary goal(s) or purpose(s). Some are listed with the set of values that a company is committed to, while others include what the company will do to reach its goals. These core goals, values, and purposes don't usually change. Answer these questions with a partner.

1. Sometimes mission statements are only one line and capture the company's core purpose or goal, such as those for Walt Disney, Wal-Mart, and Merck (a pharmaceutical company). Can you guess which is which?

    To give ordinary folk the chance to buy the same things as rich people

    _____

    To preserve and improve human life _____

    To make people happy _____

    Were they easy to figure out? Do you think one line is enough or do you think the mission statements should be longer?

    _____

    _____

    _____

2. Mission statements are not only for companies. What other kinds of organizations might have mission statements?

    _____

    _____

    _____

3. Colleges and universities often have mission statements. Can you think of a good mission statement for your school?

    _____

    _____

    _____

About Unit 1: Academic Reading 1

Academic Reading 1, which discusses the importance of company goals and the need to express them clearly to inspire company employees, is an original reading created using information from several business publications. The primary source was a trade book used as a textbook in many business schools: *Built to Last: Successful Habits of Visionary Companies.* The text was supplemented with content from an online magazine.

Before Reading Strategy: Skimming

Skimming is a pre-reading strategy that will help you read more quickly and with greater understanding. **Skimming is not reading.** When you skim, you are only looking quickly for some key information.

- First, check the title of the article or chapter. Notice the length of the passage. This will give you an idea of how long it will take you to read it.

- Then read the introduction, the first one or two sentences in each paragraph, and the conclusion. This will give you an idea what the reading is about and its purpose.

- Notice if there are features such as illustrations, graphs, and charts, or if there are bold or italic words that indicate key vocabulary.

- Read any questions or exercises connected to the reading.

By doing these four things, you will have an idea of the main points in the reading. Because you skimmed the reading, you are more likely to understand the reading and remember important information.

Practice Activity: Skimming

Skim Academic Reading 1, and answer the questions. Do <u>not</u> read slowly and carefully. How quickly can you find the answers?

1. The reading is _____ pages long.

    a. exactly two

    b. approximately two

    c. more than three

2. Paragraph 2 is mostly about _____.

    a. President Kennedy's goal to go to the moon

    b. how a goal is different from a mission statement

    c. the role of Congress in the moon mission

3. The reading is mostly about _____.

    a. two companies: Starbucks and Cold Stone Creamery

    b. the importance of a bold mission statement

    c. stimulating company progress

abc

Vocabulary Strategy: Keeping a Vocabulary Log

Any readers of academic texts will encounter a lot of advanced vocabulary. Most words you will already know, but some will be new. You need to know thousands of words to understand the academic texts you will have to read as a student. Because many words will be ones that you will see again in other academic readings and in other disciplines, it is important to notice them as you read and to record them in a vocabulary log.

Keeping a log is a good strategy to use to increase your vocabulary. You will have your words in a notebook and can easily retrieve the definition or notes later.

There are many ways to keep **a vocabulary log**, but it is a good idea to include columns for the vocabulary word or phrase; its definition or translation; and your use of it in a short phrase, sentence, or note that helps you remember it.

A vocabulary log is included in every unit of this textbook (see pages 29–30 for an example), and a blank one appears and in Appendix A, but you may also want to keep a separate notebook reserved for vocabulary. Each person's log will be unique. A sample vocabulary log entry might look like this:

Vocabulary Item	Definition or Translation	Your Original Phrase, Sentence, or Note
immense	very large	an immense problem

Practice Activity: Keeping a Vocabulary Log

Read these sentences from Academic Reading 1, and fill in the log with the underlined words. Use a dictionary for words you don't know.

1. The classic book . . . describes Boeing Corporation as an excellent example of how highly visionary companies often use <u>bold</u> missions as a particularly powerful mechanism to stimulate progress.

2. The classic book . . . describes Boeing Corporation as an excellent example of how highly visionary companies often use bold missions as a particularly powerful mechanism to stimulate <u>progress</u>.

3. The most optimistic scientific <u>assessment</u> of the moon mission's chances for success in 1961 was fifty-fifty and most experts were, in fact, more pessimistic.

4. Like the moon mission, a true goal is clear and <u>compelling</u> and serves as a unifying focal point of effort—often creating immense team spirit.

5. Like the moon mission, a true goal is clear and compelling and serves as a unifying <u>focal</u> point of effort—often creating immense team spirit.

Vocabulary Item	Definition or Translation	Your Original Phrase, Sentence, or Note
bold		
progress		
assessment		
compelling		
focal		

Vocabulary Power

There are a number of terms and phrases in this reading that you may encounter in other academic settings. Add at least five vocabulary items to your vocabulary notebook or log.

Match the words in bold from the reading on the left with a definition on the right.

_____ 1. But there is a difference between merely having a goal and becoming committed to a huge, **daunting** challenge—like a big mountain to climb.

_____ 2. The most **optimistic** scientific assessment of the moon mission's chances for success in 1961 was fifty-fifty and most experts were, in fact, more pessimistic.

_____ 3. But that's part of what made it such a powerful mechanism for getting the United States, still groggy from the 1950s and the Eisenhower era, moving **vigorously** forward.

_____ 4. Like the moon mission, a true goal is clear and compelling and serves as a unifying focal point of effort—often creating **immense** team spirit.

_____ 5. Like the moon mission, a true goal is clear and compelling and serves as a **unifying** focal point of effort—often creating immense team spirit.

_____ 6. It is **tangible**, energizing, highly focused. People "get it" right away; it takes little or no explanation.

_____ 7. It's a way to define a company's **destiny**.

_____ 8. Whether a company has the right goal or whether the goal gets people going in the right direction are not **irrelevant** questions, but they miss the essential point.

a. unimportant; unconnected

b. bringing together

c. future

d. positive

e. with strong energy

f. frightening

g. concrete; real

h. huge

Academic Reading 1

Now, read the passage. Put an X next to the lines that have information you aren't sure you understand. You will use these when you practice the After Reading Strategy on page 11.

Setting Bold Goals and Missions

1   The classic book *Built to Last: Successful Habits of Visionary Companies*[1] describes Boeing Corporation as an excellent example of how highly visionary companies often use bold missions as a particularly powerful mechanism to stimulate progress. A bold mission is not the only powerful mechanism for stimulating progress, nor do all the visionary companies use it extensively.

2   All companies have goals. But there is a difference between merely having a goal and becoming committed to a huge, daunting challenge—like a big mountain to climb. Think of the moon mission in the 1960s. President Kennedy and his advisers could have gone into a conference room and drafted something like, "Let's beef up our space program" or some other vacuous statement. The most optimistic scientific assessment of the moon mission's chances for success in 1961 was fifty-fifty and most experts were, in fact, more pessimistic.[2] Yet, nonetheless, Congress agreed (to the tune of an immediate $549 million and billions more in the following five years) with Kennedy's proclamation on May 25, 1961, "that this Nation should commit itself to achieving the goal, before this decade is out, of landing a man on the moon and returning him safely to earth."[3] Given the odds, such a bold commitment was, at the time, outrageous. But that's part of what made it such a powerful mechanism for getting the United States, still groggy from the 1950s and the Eisenhower era, moving vigorously forward.[4] According to a 2008 *Bloomberg Businessweek* article by Carmine Galo, a "communications coach for the world's most admired brands," "Scientists may have rolled their eyes after Kennedy's announcement, but they got to work on it."[5]

---

1. James C. Collins and Jerry I. Porras (New York: Harper Collins, 1997), 83–84.
2. Daniel J. Boorstin, *The Americans: The Democratic Experience* (New York: Vintage Books, 1974), 593–597.
3. Ibid., p. 596.
4. Collins and Porras, p. 94.
5. Carmine Gallo, "Building Bold Goals for Your Business," www.bloomberg.com, 2008.

3 Like the moon mission, a true goal is clear and compelling and serves as a unifying focal point of effort—often creating immense team spirit. It has a clear finish line, so the organization can know when it has achieved the goal; people like to shoot for finish lines.

4 It engages people—it reaches out and grabs them in the gut. It is tangible, energizing, highly focused. People "get it" right away; it takes little or no explanation. It's a way to define a company's destiny.

5 The moon mission didn't need a committee to spend endless hours wordsmithing the goal into a verbose, meaningless, impossible-to-remember "mission statement." No, the goal itself—the mountain to climb—was so easy to grasp, so compelling in its own right, that it could be said one hundred different ways, yet easily understood by everyone. When an expedition sets out to climb Mount Everest, it doesn't need a three-page, convoluted "mission statement" to explain what Mount Everest is. . . . Most corporate statements . . . do little to provoke forward movement (although some do help to preserve the core).[6]

6 Whether a company has the right goal or whether the goal gets people going in the right direction are not irrelevant questions, but they miss the essential point. Indeed, the *essential* point is better captured in such questions as, Does it stimulate forward progress? Does it create momentum? Does it get people going? Does it get people's juices flowing? Do they find it stimulating, exciting, adventurous? Are they willing to throw their creative talents and human energies into it? Also, does it fit with our core ideology?[7]

7 According to *Bloomberg Businessweek,* "Everything starts with a vision: finding a good hire, motivating a team, or creating a successful sales presentation. . . . Inspiring leaders frame the vision around a grand purpose. Express goals that enlarge people's vision." Starbucks Chief Executive Howard Schultz has spoken about how the company began as "a small Seattle store selling coffee beans." But that wasn't enough for Schultz. After a trip to Italy, Schultz was "determined to create a 'third place' between work and home. . . . He wanted to take the company to places others never thought possible."[8]

---

6. Collins and Porras, pp. 94–95.
7. Ibid., pp. 96–97.
8. Gallo, 2008.

8   The *Businessweek* article continues with a story about Cold Stone Creamery CEO Doug Ducey and his idea about the power of a big vision: "In 1999, Cold Stone had 74 stores. Ducey wanted to expand to 1,000 stores in five years, an ambitious goal by anyone's standards. According to Ducey, his goal had little power to inspire. But his vision [which became the mission]—to create the ultimate ice cream experience—did. . . . Whether it's . . . coffee, ice cream, or any other product or service, a bold vision sets momentum in motion. It instills confidence and unleashes the potential in . . . your team. Think big and put . . . your business on the map."[9]

---

9. Ibid., 2008.

FYI: Understanding Footnotes, Part 1

Many academic works use information from other experts or publications. When this happens, the author needs to let the reader know the material has another source.

As a reader, you need to recognize when the author is giving credit to another source. Sometimes these are done using in-text citations (which are explained on page 78), and sometimes they are done using footnotes, as on the bottom of page 8.

The information in a bibliographic footnote is similar to what is found in the complete bibliographic entry (see also page 78). The footnote usually includes the name of the author whose work is being cited, the work being cited, the publisher (if it's from a book), the year the material was published, and the page(s) from the original source if available. Sometimes the city of the publisher is listed as well.

If the source is a magazine or journal article, the name of the publication is included with the volume or issue number.

If it's an online article, the name of the website and the web address are usually included.

The word *Ibid* is sometimes used in footnotes, as shown on page 8. **Ibid** means that the exact same source as the previous one is being cited again. The footnote sometimes includes a different page number than the previous footnote.

Understanding footnotes will help you do additional research when you need to write your own paper or find other sources on the same topic.

After Reading Strategy: Re-Reading

Re-reading is one of the most popular strategies readers use when they are reading a difficult text or are struggling to understand a new concept. Re-reading does not always mean reading the entire passage again. Rather, it means going back to the part of the text where you stopped understanding and trying to read it again. Sometimes this means you only need to re-read a sentence, but sometimes you may need to start again at the beginning to discover where you stopped understanding.

When you re-read, you usually read something more slowly, and often it's just a matter of slowing down that makes the text easier to understand the next time. Also, because you have read the content once, you now already know basically where the reading is going and already understand some parts of it, which means you are just filling in the pieces instead of attempting a global understanding.

Re-reading also helps with vocabulary because you already know which words you don't know and so you are prepared when you read them the next time, meaning you can now focus on looking more at the context to see if it will help you understand unfamiliar words.

Remember that re-reading does not just mean reading something one more time. For some readings, you may need to read different parts three or four times. Don't get discouraged!

It is difficult to know in advance what parts or how much you will have to re-read. Every piece of text will be different.

Practice Activity: Re-Reading

Re-read Academic Reading 1 in its entirety. This time, read more slowly and deliberately. On this second pass through the reading, if you find that you understand something now that you didn't understand before, erase the X in the margin or cross it out.

1. Re-read again the lines/sections that still have X marks in the margin. If necessary, go back a sentence or two to try to get more of a context for the parts you don't understand.

2. If some of the items you did not understand are related to the field of business, ask your teacher or go online to find out more information to help you understand.

Practice Activity: Reading for the Big Picture

Choose the best answer to each question.

1. What is the main idea of the passage?

    a. A mission statement needs to be easily understood and motivate progress.

    b. Having the right goal is the most important thing to consider.

    c. All companies have goals to achieve and challenges to overcome.

    d. A true challenge doesn't have a clear finish line, so people keep trying to achieve it.

2. What is the essential point about having a bold goal?

    a. It is achievable.

    b. It is the right goal for the company.

    c. It prevents over-stimulation.

    d. It inspires people to invest creativity and energy.

Summarizing What You Have Read

Summarize the main points of the original sentence without re-using too many words or phrases from the original.

1. A bold mission is not the only powerful mechanism for stimulating progress, nor do all the visionary companies use it extensively.

   _____

   _____

   _____

2. The moon mission didn't need a committee to spend endless hours wordsmithing the goal into a verbose, meaningless impossible-to-remember "mission statement."

   _____

   _____

   _____

3. Whether a company has the right goal or whether the goal gets people going in the right direction are not irrelevant questions, but they miss the essential point.

   _____

   _____

   _____

Part 2: Core Values, Vision, and Purpose

Getting Started

For most successful companies, the main purpose doesn't change for many years, but the business strategies adapt and change over time based on the needs of the market. For example, Sony, a technology company, has kept the same purpose: "to experience the joy of advancing and applying technology for the benefit of the public." However, Sony's products have changed over the years, and it is likely that the way it markets each new product has evolved. Answer these questions with a partner.

1. Brainstorm a list of companies you are familiar with. Guess what each company's mission or purpose is.

   _____

   _____

   _____

   _____

2. Review the list of organizations you talked about in Part 1 (page 2). Do you think they can keep their core purpose for an extended period of time? Why or why not?

   _____

   _____

   _____

3. In what ways might the organizations you talked about in Part 1 (page 2) change their business strategies to adapt to changing times and products without changing their core purpose?

   _____

   _____

   _____

   _____

About Unit 1: Academic Reading 2

Academic Reading 2 is also an original reading created from excerpts from *Built to Last* and supplemented with information from a few other business sources. It builds on the information from Reading 1 about goals and missions and talks about strategic planning and developing core purposes.

Before Reading Strategy: Determining What You Already Know

Thinking about what they might already know about a topic is something good readers do before they read. You probably have some knowledge, however small, about almost every topic that you read about. It is a helpful strategy because by thinking about what you already know, you are in a good position to know what you don't know—or what is new to you on a topic. **Determining what you know** will help you learn new information more effectively, focus on the topic, and comprehend what you read more easily. Here are some things that will help you.

1. Make sure you know the topic of the reading before you begin. **Check the title and any introductory information.** Skim the reading.

2. Take a few minutes to **think about the topic and what you already know**. It is sometimes useful to talk to a classmate, both because you can put your thoughts into words and hear what your classmate already knows. However, even if you don't have a partner, this is an important step. When you do this, think about what you have heard or read on the topic, general impressions you might have of it, or questions or thoughts you might have, such as, "I've heard people talk about missions, but I don't think I know how they apply in business."

3. **Think about the vocabulary that might be related to the topic and that you might see in the text.** Which words and phrases do you already know and associate with that topic? Is there any vocabulary you know in a language other than English? Consider finding words in a bilingual dictionary before you read.

Practice Activity: What Do You Already Know?

Answer the questions in preparation for Academic Reading 2. Read the title, and skim the reading before you answer the questions. Then talk with a classmate to compare answers and learn more about the topic.

1. Yes   No   I understand the phrase *core ideology*.

2. Yes   No   I have seen one or both of these words (*core* and *ideology*) before and know what it means/what they mean?

3. Yes   No   I know what a *vision* is and understand why it is important.

4. Yes   No   I think I understand why companies talk about their visions and purposes.

5. Yes   No   I know what a *purpose* is and how values influence it.

6. Yes   No   I am familiar with one or two of the companies listed in the chart on page 23 and know what their business is.

7. Yes   No   I have heard the words *core ideology*, *vision*, and *purpose*.

8. Yes   No   I know how the words *core ideology*, *vision*, and *purpose* relate to the topic.

During Reading Strategy: Annotating as You Read

Annotating is basically summarizing the most important information in each paragraph as you read by making notes. You cannot summarize without understanding what you've read, so it is a useful way to check comprehension. In addition, you are creating a useful study guide that you can use when you participate in class discussions and study for tests. You can write your notes in the margin or on sticky notes. You can also circle, highlight, or underline main ideas and definitions.

You might want to note the purpose of some paragraphs; for example, you could mark a story used to explain a point as "example" or "ex." An example of how Paragraph 1 of Academic Reading 2 could be annotated is shown.

. . . the fundamental distinguishing characteristic of the
most enduring and successful corporations is that they
preserve a (cherished) *valued* core ideology while simultaneously
stimulating progress and change in everything that is
not part of their core ideology. Put another way, they
distinguish their timeless core values and enduring
core purpose (which should never change) from their
operating practices and business strategies (which
should be changing constantly in response to a
changing world). In truly great companies, change *is* a
constant, but not the *only* constant. They understand
the difference between what should never change and
what should be open for change, between what is truly
(sacred) and what is not. And by being clear about what
should never change, they are better able to stimulate
change and progress in everything else.

Margin annotations:

- fund char.—keep core ideology, start progress
- value & purpose—never change
- strategies—always changing
- great companies know the diff.
- sacred = something held dear, same as cherished

Practice Activity: Annotating

Read the sentences from another source about businesses, and practice annotating important ideas and vocabulary. What did you highlight and circle? Compare your annotations with a partner.

1. People always look at the leader when they want to take the pulse of an organization. Setting a good example says a lot. Do they see a boss they can believe in? Can they have faith in whom they follow? Commitment climbs when people see passion in the person out front. They catch the feeling. Commitment is a highly contagious thing. It carries a mental magnetism that captures the attention and enlists the energies of those who watch.

2. Commitment rarely comes without reciprocity. That is, we hardly ever get it from others without making some sort of commitments in return. As the ancient Greeks said, "Quid pro quo." You have to be invested in the staff if you want them to be invested in their work.

3. Cohesiveness—the "we" spirit within the group—can wield heavy influence on commitment. The stronger ties between the people, the more those personal bonds serve to power individual effort. You can't make camaraderie a job requirement. What you can do is encourage it and create a conducive environment that helps it happen spontaneously.

Vocabulary Power

There are a number of terms and phrases in this reading that you may encounter in other academic settings. Add at least five vocabulary items to your vocabulary notebook or log.

Match the words in bold from the reading on the left with a definition on the right.

_____ 1. To pursue the vision means to create organizational and strategic alignment to preserve the core **ideology** and stimulate progress toward the envisioned future.

_____ 2. Leaders die, products become **obsolete**, markets change, new technologies emerge, management fads come and go; but core ideology in a great company endures as a source of guidance and inspiration.

_____ 3. Leaders die, products become obsolete, markets change, new technologies emerge, management fads come and go; but core ideology in a great company **endures** as a source of guidance and inspiration.

_____ 4. Leaders die, products become obsolete, markets change, new technologies emerge, management fads come and go; but core ideology in a great company endures as a source of guidance and **inspiration**.

_____ 5. Core ideology provides the bonding glue that holds an organization together as it grows, decentralizes, diversifies, expands globally, and **attains** diversity within.

_____ 6. Many experts agree that if the purpose tries to claim a value not universally accepted by employees—that is, if it's not considered **authentic**—then the purpose will not be taken seriously.

_____ 7. . . . an **aspiration** to do something that can be briefly achieved but impossible to sustain (such as curing cancer).

_____ 8. To provide a place for people to **flourish** and to enhance the community

a. objective

b. real; not false

c. gains or achieves

d. set of shared beliefs

e. lasts

f. way to motivate

g. old-fashioned; no longer in use

h. grow; succeed

Academic Reading 2

Now, read the passage.

The Importance of the Right Purpose

1   *In Build to Last,*[1] Collins and Porras claim that the fundamental distinguishing characteristic of the most enduring and successful corporations is that they preserve a cherished core ideology while simultaneously stimulating progress and change in everything that is not part of their core ideology. Put another way, they distinguish their timeless core values and enduring core purpose (which should never change) from their operating practices and business strategies (which should be changing constantly in response to a changing world). In truly great companies, change *is* a constant, but not the *only* constant. They understand the difference between what should never change and what should be open for change, between what is truly sacred and what is not. And by being clear about what should never change, they are better able to stimulate change and progress in everything else.

The Vision Framework

2   A well-conceived vision consists of two major components— *core ideology* and an *envisioned future.* Notice the direct parallel to the fundamental "preserve the core/ stimulate progress" dynamic. A good vision builds on the interplay between these two complementary yin-and-yang forces: it defines "what we stand for and why we exist" that does not change

---

1. *Built to Last: Successful Habits of Visionary Companies,* James Collins and Jerry I. Porras (New York: Harper Collins, 1994), p. 220.

(the core ideology) and sets forth "what we aspire to become, to achieve, to create" that will require significant change and progress to attain (the envisioned future).

3   To pursue the vision means to create organizational and strategic alignment to preserve the core ideology and stimulate progress toward the envisioned future. Alignment brings the vision to life, translating it from good intentions to concrete reality.[2]

Core Ideology

4   Core ideology defines the enduring character of an organization— its self-identity that remains consistent through time and transcends product/ market life cycles, technological breakthroughs, management fads, and individual leaders. In fact, the most lasting and significant contribution of the architects of visionary companies *is* the core ideology. . . . Leaders die, products become obsolete, markets change, new technologies emerge, management fads come and go; but core ideology in a great company endures as a source of guidance and inspiration.

5   Core ideology provides the bonding glue that holds an organization together as it grows, decentralizes, diversifies, expands globally, and attains diversity within. Think of core ideology like the truths held to be "self-evident" in the United States Declaration of Independence, or the enduring ideals and principles of the scientific community that bond scientists from every nationality together with the common purpose of advancing human knowledge. Any effective vision must embody the core ideology of the organization, which in turn consists of two distinct sub-components: core values and core purpose.[3]

Core Values

6   Core values are the organ- ization's essential and enduring tenets—a small set of timeless guiding principles that require no external justification; they have *intrinsic* value and importance to those inside the organization. Disney's core values of imagination and wholesomeness stem not from a market requirement, but from an inner belief that imagination and wholesomeness should be nurtured for their own sake. . . . Ralph Larson, CEO of Johnson & Johnson, put it this way: "The core values embodied in our credo might be a competitive advantage, but that is not *why* we have them. We have them because they

2. Ibid., pp. 220–221.
3. Ibid., p. 221.

define for us what we stand for, and we would hold them even if they became a competitive *dis*advantage in certain situations."[4]

7   The key point is that an enduring great company decides *for itself* what values it holds to be core, largely independent of the current environment, competitive requirements, or management fads. Clearly, then, there is no universally "right" set of core values. A company need not have customer service as a core value (Sony doesn't), or respect for the individual (Disney doesn't), or quality (Wal-Mart doesn't), or market responsiveness (Hewlett Packard doesn't), or team-work (Nordstrom doesn't). Again, to emphasize a fundamental finding of our research, the key is not *what* core values an organization has, but *that it has* core values.[5]

Core Purpose

8   According to several business sources including the Internet Center for Management and Business Administration (ICMBA), a core purpose is idealistic and describes a "reason for being. . . . Initial attempts at stating a core purpose often result in

too specific of a statement that focuses on a product or service. To isolate the core purpose, it is useful to ask 'why' in response to product-oriented statements."[6]

9   The ICMBA site also discusses how values influence the purpose: "The core purpose and values of the firm are not selected—they are discovered. The stated ideology should not be a goal or aspiration but rather, it should portray the firm as it really."[7] Many experts agree that if the purpose tries to claim a value not universally accepted by employees—that is, if it's not considered authentic—then the purpose will not be taken seriously.

10   So how does a company define an idealistic "reason for being" or an organizational greater purpose? According to Smith and Glynn of the University of Michigan Ross School of Business, "It serves to attract people . . . in a deeply human way. It guides the formation of the organizational vision and mission statements strategically by separating the organization from the competitive landscape (for example, 'We will not be distracted by the latest fads; we will stay true to our purpose'), guiding resources toward an articulated

---

4. Ibid., p. 222.
5. Ibid., p. 221.
6. ICMBA, www.quickmba.com, 2010.
7. Ibid.

purpose ('Is this use of resources consistent with our core purpose'), and by laying the foundations of a clear corporate culture ('We are about X. If that resonates with you, join us and together we can try to accomplish it')."[8]

11   Smith and Glynn say such a statement includes three primary items: (1) the meeting of a need to make the world a "better place"; (2) provision of goods and/or services that society wants; and (3) an aspiration to do something that can be briefly achieved but impossible to sustain (such as curing cancer). This last item, say Smith and Glynn, "is what weaves the purpose statement into the enduring identity of the organization. As other objectives, goals, and contexts shift and change, a greater purpose statement with its aspirations can last in a way that provides stability and consistency (for example, Merck strives to preserve and improve human life; Walt Disney strives to make people happy, etc.)."[9] Table 1 shows some examples of core purpose.

Table 1. Example of Core Purpose	
3M	To solve unsolved problems
Cargill	To improve the standard of living around the world
Cold Stone Creamery	We will make people happy.
CVS Corporation	To be easiest pharmacy retailer for customers to use
Darden Restaurants	To nourish and delight everyone we serve
Fannie Mae	To strengthen the social fabric by continually democratizing home ownership
FARMCO	To provide innovative agricultural solutions to farmers to overcome starvation and malnourishment around the world
Geico	To provide excellent coverage, low prices, and outstanding service
Google	To organize the world's information and make it universally accessible and useful
Hewlett-Packard	To make technical contributions for the advancement and welfare of humanity
Mary Kay	To give unlimited opportunity to women
Pacific Theatres	To provide a place for people to flourish and to enhance the community
Starbucks	To inspire and nurture the human spirit—one person, one cup, and one neighborhood at a time
Telecare	To help people with mental impairments realize their full potential

---

8. Brandon Mikel Smith and Mary Ann Glynn, "Leading with a Purpose: Fueling the Human Spirit in Times of Uncertainty," www.bus.umich.edu/positive/pos-research/, 2012.
9. Ibid.

After Reading Strategy: Summarizing

Summarizing means identifying the main points of the reading and stating them in your own words. If you can summarize a reading, you know you have understood it.

How detailed your summary is depends on your purpose for reading. For example, if you are reading for background information, a basic summary will be enough. If you need to understand the reading's main ideas and be able to explain examples to prepare for a discussion or a test, your summary should be more detailed. In either case, a summary is much shorter than the original.

Your annotations will be very useful for writing your summary because they should already express the main ideas in your own words.

Practice Activity: Summarizing

Work with a partner.

1. Take turns. Re-read your annotation for one paragraph from the reading. Then cover it up. Re-state the points in your own words. Your partner will compare your version with his or her version.

2. Take turns. Explain the purpose of each paragraph in Academic Reading 2. Use phrases such as *It explains the importance of . . . , It describes the concept of . . . ,* or *It gives an example of. . . .*

3. Think about the information in each paragraph in Academic Reading 2. Which paragraphs show essential information to understanding the main points of the reading?

_____

_____

Practice Activity: Reading for the Big Picture

Write T if the statement is true or F if the statement is false.

1. _____ Companies constantly change their core purpose to stimulate progress.

2. _____ A strong vision has two parts: core ideology and envisioned future.

3. _____ Core values are timeless and are important to those who work for the company.

4. _____ A core purpose should not be the company's reason for being.

5. _____ The core purpose and values are carefully selected.

6. _____ The company's purpose doesn't change with the goals.

Summarizing What You Have Read

Summarize the main points of the original without re-using too many words or phrases from the original.

1. To pursue the vision means to create organizational and strategic alignment to preserve the core ideology and stimulate progress toward the envisioned future.

   _____

   _____

   _____

   _____

2. Leaders die, products become obsolete, markets change, new technologies emerge, management fads come and go; but core ideology in a great company endures as a source of guidance and inspiration.

   _____

   _____

   _____

   _____

3. Core ideology provides the bonding glue that holds an organization together as it grows, decentralizes, diversifies, expands globally, and attains diversity within.

   _____

   _____

   _____

   _____

Your Active Vocabulary in the Real World

Vocabulary is important. Some words are useful for your speaking or for your writing, but other words are useful for your reading or your listening. For each word, decide how you think you will probably need this word for your English. Put a check mark (✓) under the ways you think you are likely to need the word. It is possible to have a check mark in more than one column.

	YOUR VOCABULARY	I need to be able to use this word in WRITING.	I need to be able to use this word in SPEAKING.	I need to understand this word in READING.	I need to understand this word in LISTENING.
1.	adapt				
2.	figure out				
3.	an era				
4.	a focal point				
5.	irrelevant				
6.	ordinary				
7.	put another way				
8.	contagious				
9.	a component				
10.	customer service				

Rapid Vocabulary Review

From the three answers on the right, circle the one that best explains, is an example of, or combines with the vocabulary word on the left as it is used in this unit.

Vocabulary	Answers		
Synonyms			
1. steady	heavy	consistent	focused
2. enhance	cover	feature	improve
3. essential	necessary	problematic	suspicious
4. capture	break	catch	protect
5. component	a method	a question	an ingredient
6. achieve	accomplish	delete	argue
7. convoluted	simplistic	complicated	unintelligible
8. grand	glorious	modest	trivial
9. staff	furniture	rules	workers
10. the source	the origin	the limit	the result
11. ultimate	eventual	maximum	largest
12. pessimistic	angry	impossible	negative
Combinations and Associations			
13. put another ___	day	say	way
14. ___ return	in	on	with
15. ___ forth	like	open	set
16. in ___	move	proud	turn
17. consist ___	in	of	with
18. beef ___	up	in	over
19. ___ intentions	dull	good	happy
20. wield ___	friendship	influence	religion

Vocabulary Log

To increase your vocabulary knowledge, write a definition or translation for each vocabulary item. Then write an original phrase, sentence, or note that will help you remember the vocabulary item.

Vocabulary Item	Definition or Translation	Your Original Phrase, Sentence, or Note
1. adapt	to adjust or modify	Animals adapt to their environment.
2. figure out		
3. extensively		
4. core		
5. pursue		
6. outrageous		
7. require		
8. technique		
9. tangible		
10. isolate		
11. irrelevant		
12. folk		
13. fundamental		
14. simultaneously		

Vocabulary Item	Definition or Translation	Your Original Phrase, Sentence, or Note
15. pulse		
16. contagious		
17. spontaneously		
18. staff		
19. enlist		
20. cherish		
21. stimulate		
22. preserve		
23. envision		
24. provoke		
25. attain		

2 Architecture: The Hoover Dam

There are about 90,000 dams in the world. Dams are structures that hold back large amounts of water. Dams are not a new concept. There were dams in Mesopotamia, ancient Egypt, and early Rome. Some dams are built by animals, such as beavers, some are constructed by humans, and some are formed by natural causes. Dams are classified several ways: size, purpose, structure, and/or material. The readings in this unit examine one important dam: the Hoover Dam in the United States.

Part 1: Public Projects

Getting Started

One famous dam in the United States, the Hoover Dam, is located on the border between the states of Arizona and Nevada. The dam of the Colorado River took five years to build, from 1931 to 1936, but was dedicated in 1935. Answer these questions with a partner.

1. Have you ever seen a dam? What dams are you familiar with? Where are they?

   _____

   _____

   _____

   _____

2. Dams hold a lot of water. Some dams are used to generate electricity. What other purposes might dams serve?

   _____

   _____

   _____

   _____

About Unit 2: Academic Reading 1

Academic Reading 1 is from a reference book titled *How Stuff Works*. This type of book often provides background information on a topic for general readers. The passage discusses the Hoover Dam and some consequences if the dam broke. It explores what would happen to the surrounding areas as well as what would happen to the dam itself.

Before Reading Strategy: Knowing the Purpose for Reading

Academic readings can be long and challenging. Sometimes it is hard to motivate yourself to read, especially in a field that is different than your own or does not seem relevant to your life. It can be helpful to develop **a goal,** or **purpose,** for your reading. By working toward the goal, you will focus on the reading achieving the goal. Always make sure that you know **why** you are reading the text and **what** information you need (or want) to learn before you start reading.

Purposes can vary:

- It may be a purpose **from the teacher,** such as learning something that may appear later on a test or gathering information to complete a writing assignment.
- It may be a purpose **from the textbook,** such as meeting the objectives listed at the beginning of a chapter.
- It may be a purpose **from your advisor,** such as background reading.

Knowing the purpose before you start may also save you time in the long run. Motivate yourself by asking questions about the topic that you hope to answer or questions that you want to ask during class. You can also make predictions about the topic and track how many you get right. Setting goals helps you pay more attention to the information you need, rather than trying to remember every single detail.

Practice Activity: Knowing the Purpose for Reading

Academic Reading 1 discusses what would happen if one of the United States' most important water delivery systems failed. Focus on the topic by answering these questions.

1. What objectives does your instructor have for asking you to read this?

   _____

2. What do you need to learn from this reading? _____

   _____

3. Why do you think the author chose to write about this topic? Give at least two reasons. _____

   _____

   _____

abc

Vocabulary Strategy: Identifying Synonyms

When you learn a new word, you should also learn a synonym or two for it. One of your first questions might be, "I already know a similar word for that idea. How is this new word different from the word I already know?" Or, you may not know another word that is similar. Learning synonyms is extremely useful in increasing your vocabulary and overall fluency. It will greatly help your reading, speaking, listening, and writing.

Knowing a lot of synonyms is also very helpful when you are paraphrasing. You should begin to notice that some words are related but not exact synonyms. For example, the word *commerce* means "business." A thesaurus might use a word like *trade* because that also means "business." A good thesaurus would also list *dealings* and *retailing* as related words because they don't have the exact meaning. Some thesauruses (and dictionaries) make this distinction. When you choose to paraphrase, you should make sure the word or words you are using mean the same thing as the original does.

Practice Activity: Identifying Synonyms

Do you know any synonyms for these words? If not, use a dictionary to identify one or two synonyms for each of these words from Academic Reading 1.

modern   _____   _____

amazing   _____   _____

effect   _____   _____

quickly   _____   _____

represent   _____   _____

sizable   _____   _____

Vocabulary Power

There are a number of terms and phrases in this reading that you may encounter in other academic settings. Add at least five vocabulary items to your vocabulary notebook or log.

Match the words in bold from the reading on the left with a definition on the right.

_____ 1. The Hoover Dam is one of those miracles of the modern world that almost **defies** explanation

_____ 2. No **conventional** bomb would have an effect on a dam like this.

_____ 3. But let's say that some sort of tremendous earthquake or an asteroid strike or some other natural disaster were to somehow **eliminate** the Hoover Dam in one fell swoop.

_____ 4. If you eliminated a sizable amount of generating **capacity** like that . . . .

_____ 5. Farmers in the Imperial Valley get most of their water from the Colorado River, and these irrigation systems would **collapse**.

_____ 6. Prior to irrigation, the Imperial Valley was a **barren** desert.

_____ 7. With the loss of water and the loss of power, Las Vegas would become uninhabitable, and that would **displace** 1.5 million residents and empty more than 120,000 hotels rooms and the casinos, bringing the multi-billion-dollar gambling industry in this city to a halt.

_____ 8. With the loss of water and the loss of power, Las Vegas would become uninhabitable, and that would displace 1.5 million residents and empty more than 120,000 hotels rooms and the casinos, bringing the multi-billion-dollar gambling industry in this city to a **halt**.

a. usual

b. ability

c. complete stop

d. fail; come to nothing

e. resists

f. get rid of

g. cause to relocate

h. empty

Academic Reading 1

Now, read the passage.

What If the Hoover Dam Broke?

1   The Hoover Dam is one of those miracles of the modern world that almost defies explanation. When you stand next to it, the size is unbelievable. It is more than 700 feet high (imagine a 70-story building). The top of the dam is more than 1,200 feet long. At the base, it is an amazing 660 feet thick and at the top it is 45 feet thick. The water on the lake side is more than 500 feet deep, and the lake holds a total of 10 trillion or so gallons of water—enough water to cover a state like Connecticut 10 feet deep.

2   Let's say the Hoover Dam broke. This is difficult to imagine, given its thickness. No conventional bomb would have an effect on a dam like this. It is difficult to imagine even a nuclear bomb having an effect, unless it were an extremely powerful one and it were inside the dam at the time of explosion. But let's say that some sort of tremendous earthquake or an asteroid strike or some other natural disaster were to somehow eliminate the Hoover Dam in one fell swoop. What would happen?

3   The first thing that would happen is that 10 trillion gallons of water would move as quickly as they could out of the lake and down the river in a huge tsunami of water. The Hoover Dam is located in a desert area that is not hugely inhabited below the dam, but there are still some sizable populations. Lake Havasu City, population 40,000, is about the biggest town in the United States along the river. Bullhead City, population 30,000, is also close to the dam. Needles (California), Blythe (California), and Laughlin (Nevada) all have populations of around 10,000 people as well.

4   Where the water would do immense damage is in the lakes below the Hoover Dam. It turns out that below the Hoover Dam is another large lake called Lake Mohave, which is held in place by Davis Dam, and below that is Lake Havasu, held in place by Parker Dam. These are smaller lakes and smaller dams. For example, Lake Havasu only holds about 200 billion gallons of water.

5   As the water released by the Hoover Dam moved through these two lakes, it would likely destroy them and their dams as well. That's where the real impact would be felt, because these lakes affect a huge number of people. The water in them produces hydro-electric power, irrigates farmland, and supplies drinking water to cities like Los Angeles, Las Vegas, Phoenix, and San Diego.

6   The Hoover Dam produces roughly 2,000 megawatts of power. Davis and Parker Dams produce less, but together they might all produce 3,000 megawatts. That represents about one half of one percent of the total electrical power produced in the United States. If you eliminated a sizable amount of generating capacity like that, especially in that area of the country (near Los Angeles and Las Vegas, for example), it would definitely cause problems.

7   The destruction of irrigation water supplies would also have a huge effect on farming in the region. Farmers in the Imperial Valley get most of their water from the Colorado River, and these irrigation systems would collapse. Prior to irrigation, the Imperial Valley was a barren desert. Today it is the home of more than half a million acres of farmland and produces more than a billion dollars in fruits and vegetables every year.

8   There would be large effects as well from the loss of drinking water. For example, Las Vegas gets 85 percent of its drinking water from Lake Mead—the lake behind Hoover Dam. With the loss of water and the loss of power, Las Vegas would become uninhabitable, and that would displace 1.5 million residents and empty more than 120,000 hotels rooms and the casinos, bringing the multi-billion-dollar gambling industry in this city to a halt.

9   Isn't it amazing how much commerce and how many people depend on one dam?

After Reading Strategy: Understanding Details

Sometimes, the purpose of reading certain academic texts is to learn some specific facts or statistics about a topic to help develop your understanding of an event or a concept. When that is a purpose of your reading, you will probably want to go back through the text several times to make sure you have understood all of the **important details.**

Some textbooks give the impression that details aren't important, but that is not true. Again, it depends on the purpose. For much of the academic reading you will do, it will be most important to understand the main ideas, but for others, the details will be important, especially if you need to write about it later or answer questions on a test. Details are more likely to be important when reading about historical events, scientific experiments, literature, mathematical equations, or processes.

If understanding the details is an important component of your reading task, you will want to review the text more than once. **Details are often names, places, numbers, and/or dates.** Read carefully for these types of details.

Practice Activity: Understanding Details

Assume that your purpose for reading about the Hoover Dam was to understand details. Answer the questions.

1. What are the three most important pieces of specific information given about the dam in Paragraph 1?

   _____

   _____

   _____

2. What other dams would be affected if the Hoover Dam broke?

   _____

3. Which cities would lose power and drinking water if the Hoover Dam broke and severely damaged Davis and Parker Dams?

_____

4. In which area would farmland be most negatively impacted if the Hoover Dam broke?

_____

5. Which city would suffer the most damage if the Hoover Dam broke?

_____

Practice Activity: Reading for the Big Picture

Although the last activity focused on details, this one focuses on main ideas. Choose the best answer for each question.

1. What is the main idea of the passage?

   a. If the Hoover Dam broke, it would be the result of a natural disaster or a bomb.

   b. If the Hoover Dam broke, surrounding cities would suffer.

   c. If the Hoover Dam broke, cities and other dams would be damaged.

   d. If the Hoover Dam broke, people would not have enough drinking water.

2. Which events would happen if the Hoover Dam broke? Choose all that are correct.

   a. an earthquake would be triggered

   b. a tsunami would be triggered

   c. electricity could not be generated at the same capacity

   d. farmers would not need to irrigate for a long time

   e. the fruit and vegetable industry would suffer

   f. drinking water would be lost

   g. people would have to move to Las Vegas

Summarizing What You Have Read

Summarize the main points of the original sentence without re-using too many words or phrases from the original.

1. It is difficult to imagine even a nuclear bomb having an effect, unless it were an extremely powerful one and it were inside the dam at the time of explosion.

   _____

   _____

   _____

2. The first thing that would happen is that 10 trillion gallons of water would move as quickly as they could out of the lake and down the river in a huge tsunami of water.

   _____

   _____

   _____

3. If you eliminated a sizable amount of generating capacity like that, especially in that area of the country (near Los Angeles and Las Vegas, for example), it would definitely cause problems.

   _____

   _____

   _____

Part 2: Constructing the Hoover Dam

Getting Started

There are many types of dams, and they are different sizes, serve different purposes, and are made from different materials. Building dams is considered challenging and requires great engineering and architectural skills. Answer these questions with a partner.

1. Can you think of materials that would be used to make a dam?

   _____

   _____

   _____

   _____

2. What kinds of things do you think engineers and architects have to think about to build a dam?

   _____

   _____

   _____

   _____

3. Do you think you would ever want to build structures? Why or why not?

   _____

   _____

   _____

   _____

About Unit 2: Academic Reading 2

Academic Reading 2 is from a book called *Great Projects* that explores the history of engineering in the United States by looking at some of the biggest engineering projects. Unlike the source of the first reading in this unit, this type of book includes a lot of detail about various engineering projects and assumes readers want to know more specific information.

Before Reading Strategy: Preparing for a New Topic

We all have to read things on topics that are new or unfamiliar to us. As a result, it's important to know what to do when you have to read something on a topic that is new to you.

Read the title of the reading on page 46. Before you even start reading, you recognize that you are worried that you won't understand enough of the vocabulary to be able to understand the reading. What can you do?

1. Go online or to a reference book and try to find a short explanation of the topic or event. In the case of Academic Reading 2, it might be "structural engineering." In this type of source, the explanation is designed to be simple and general. It will give you a basic idea of the concepts and vocabulary. It might also provide some ideas for similar topics you could look at. Make a list of words on the topic that might appear in the reading.

2. Go online to look for photos related to the topic of the reading. Sometimes you just need to be able to get a picture in your head of a particular concept. In the case of Academic Reading 2, look again at the photos on pages 41 and 46, but also search for photos online related to the building of the Hoover Dam.

3. Skim the reading to look for vocabulary that you don't know. Make a list of the words and add them to your vocabulary log. Look up the meanings <u>before</u> you start reading. See the Vocabulary Strategy on page 5.

4. Skim the reading to look for other clues to understand what the reading is about. Talk to your classmates. Share what you think you know.

Practice Activity: Preparing for a New Topic

Prepare for the reading on pages 46–49 by answering these questions.

1. Look up *structural engineering* in a reference book or online source. What is given as the basic meaning?

   _____

   _____

2. As you read more about the topic, what are some vocabulary words that you see used more than once?

   _____

   _____

3. Skim the reading to see if you find any of the same words in the reading. If so, which ones?

   _____

   _____

4. Write a sentence about what you think the reading will be about.

   _____

   _____

abc

Vocabulary Strategy: Previewing Difficult Vocabulary

Another key to preparing for an academic reading is to make sure you know some of the vocabulary related to the topic. Even if you are an engineering student, for example, and the reading is on an engineering-related topic, there will be vocabulary you may not know or may not know in English.

To **preview vocabulary**, do some of the same things you would do to prepare for a reading on a new topic (listed on page 42). For example:

> Skim the reading to look for vocabulary you don't know. Make a list of the words and add them to your vocabulary log. Look up the meanings <u>before</u> you start reading.

If you know the meaning of the new or difficult words before you start reading, it will help improve your understanding of the reading the first time you read it. However, re-reading (see the After Reading Strategy on page 11) can also help you solidify your understanding of new vocabulary.

Practice Activity: Previewing Difficult Vocabulary

Academic Reading 2 includes a description of some of the challenges facing the engineers of the Hoover Dam. The descriptions include words and engineering concepts that you may not be familiar with. Follow these steps.

1. Circle or highlight the vocabulary items in Paragraphs 5–7 that are new to you.

2. Skim the reading, and underline the words or phrases that seem to describe the process of building the dam.

3. Look up the meanings of the vocabulary words that are unknown to you. Add them to your vocabulary log.

Vocabulary Power

There are a number of terms and phrases in this reading that you may encounter in other academic settings. Add at least five vocabulary items to your vocabulary notebook or log.

Match the words in bold from the reading on the left with a definition on the right.

_____ 1. Yet one measure of the immensity of the Hoover Dam is that the tunnels were merely a **preliminary** to the main task at hand.

_____ 2. For years, Reclamation engineers had been **pondering** what sort of wall would halt the great river in its ancient bed and hold back its immense pressure—some 45,000 pounds per square foot at the dam's base.

_____ 3. They also had to block this force of nature beyond any possibility of failure. Anything less would court **catastrophe**.

_____ 4. . . . then mixed with water and Portland cement to make a stream of **flawless** concrete that would flow without letup for four years.

_____ 5. Somehow, too, the engineers had to **outwit** the chemistry of concrete.

_____ 6. As the grout hardened, the pile of blocks **fused** into a single mass.

_____ 7. Compared to most other construction jobs, the structures still to be finished seemed **colossal**: the power plant; the soaring towers that would take in water from the reservoir; the pipes to carry water from the towers to the plant.

_____ 8. It is easy enough to **enumerate** the tangible benefits of the Hoover Dam.

a. disaster

b. perfect

c. list

d. early; first

e. thinking about

f. became one

g. huge

h. be better than

Academic Reading 2

Now, read the passage. Keep your vocabulary log open so that you can refer to it as you are reading.

Boulder Dam and Fortification Mt.

The Building of the Hoover Dam

1   The diversion of the [Colorado] river through the canyon walls ranks as one of history's great feats of engineering. Yet one measure of the immensity of the Hoover Dam (originally called the Boulder Dam) is that the tunnels were merely a preliminary to the main task at hand.

2   For years, [Bureau of] Reclamation engineers had been pondering what sort of wall would not only halt the great river in its ancient bed and hold back its immense pressure—some 45,000 pounds per square foot at the dam's base. They also had to block this force of nature beyond any possibility of failure. Anything less would court catastrophe. After considering various designs, they chose the form known as an *arch-gravity dam*. It would take the shape of an *inverted wedge*; that is, a wall thick at the bottom and thin at the top, curving into cliffs on either side. With this ingenious shape, the wall would play a kind of trick on the river, transferring the water's enormous weight through the concrete to the canyon. In other words, the water would jam the dam into place, compressing the concrete, while the dam's weight pressed down into the riverbed.

3   This was Frank Crowe's main job—to pour 4.4 million cubic yards of concrete to make a curving wall 727 feet high and 660 feet thick at the base. It would contain enough concrete to pave a standard highway from San Francisco to New York. This was not just a huge job, but a tricky one. Enormous fields of gravel had to be found nearby and excavated, then filtered to eliminate clay and organic material, and then

mixed with water and Portland cement to make a stream of flawless concrete that would flow without letup for four years. Somehow the concrete had to be carried to the dam at great speed, because the mixture required at the Hoover Dam was unusually dry to ensure it would set properly. If the gray-white mud took too long to get from the mixing plant to the dam, it would harden into uselessness en route.

4   Somehow, too, the engineers had to outwit the chemistry of concrete. If Crowe built the Hoover Dam as a single monolithic mass, it would not fully cool for more than a century. In the meantime, the earth's biggest structure, contracting as it cooled, would crack into the earth's biggest pieces.

5   There was an even bigger problem. Standard practice for a major concrete job like this required the laborious construction of tall trestles and scaffolds by which workers and trucks could get at the structure to pour the concrete. But on a job so big, this never could be done fast enough to meet [the company's] deadline. Woody Williams had faced the same sort of problem in the tunnels. To solve it, he had rigged a new machine. Crowe imagined a similar solution on a scale magnified many times. It was an open-air machine that filled the entire dam site. Inspired by devices he had made for earlier dams, Crowe wove a web of five cableways high above the canyon floor. Each cableway held six lines suspended between 90-foot towers. The towers could be pushed north or south along the canyon as needed via railroad tracks. Along the canyon-spanning cables, carriages moved back and forth, each equipped with dangling hooks for picking up and putting down great loads of anything that was needed anywhere on the site—loads of pipe, loads of men, or 8-cubic-yard buckets of concrete. In a booth on the canyon rim, an operator sat like a master of monstrous marionettes,* watching hand signals from men below [and], then sending buckets over the lines at the rate of 1,200 feet per minute, then dropping the buckets down to the precise point on the rising structure where they were needed.

marionettes: puppets

6   When the men on the dam opened the bottom-side doors in a bucket, mushy concrete weighing sixteen tons fell into a wooden form as big as a house. Men called puddlers stomped on the mushy mass to press it into place. Then another load was dumped and another until the form was full. When the form was pulled away, it left a shape like a very large child's block.

7   At first, the movements went slowly—getting the loaded buckets from the mixing plant via rail to the right spot on the canyon floor; hooking the bucket to the

proper cable line; hoisting the bucket and moving it to the pour site many yards distant; lowering it; dumping it; raising the line and moving the carriage to haul the empty bucket away and retrieve a new one. In the first month of pouring, June 1932, the crews poured only 25,000 cubic yards—far too slow to meet their timetable.

8   But week by week they developed a routine and a rhythm. Soon, the journalist Duncan Aikman observed, there was "a stark and uncompromising efficiency . . . . Everywhere men move fast, throw all their power of muscle and machinery into what they are doing, waste no time in workmanly sociabilities on the job. There is no gaiety about the scene, no sense of men colorfully enjoying their work. Instead, a kind of surly determination broods over their labor." It took just 60 days for the men to raise their speed from 25,000 cubic yards per month to nearly 150,000 yards. By March 1934, it was 262,000 yards, one huge bucket every 78 seconds.

9   A time-lapse movie of the dam in progress would show shapes rising one block at a time to form 230 towering columns, with the columns standing up against each other to form a thick wall between the canyon's cliffs. Each block was penetrated by cold-water pipes, five feet apart. Thus, one block at a time, the hot concrete cooled fast. Into the narrow cracks between the columns, Crowe's crews pumped tons of muddy grout. As the grout hardened, the pile of blocks fused into a single mass.

10   The Reclamation Bureau's original schedule set December 4, 1934, as the day when [they] should *start* pouring concrete. On December 5, 1934, the 3-millionth ton of concrete joined the dam. In a matter of weeks the wall was done. The boss had earned his nickname—"Hurry-Up" Crowe. Compared to most other construction jobs, the structures still to be finished seemed colossal: the power plant; the soaring towers that would take in water from the reservoir; the pipes to carry water from the towers to the plant. Yet compared to the dam itself, they seemed like afterthoughts. . . .

11   Gradually, the men and the Reclamation Bureau introduced the Colorado [River] to its new regime. They divided the waters and put them to work—some to turn the giant turbines in the powerhouse, some to irrigate the farms of the Imperial Valley. Much of the rest pooled behind the wall and backed up into the space that would be called Lake Mead, the largest reservoir in the United States, big enough to hold all the water that flows down the river in two years.

12   It is easy enough to enumerate the tangible benefits of the Hoover Dam. It became the keystone in a system of dams and canals that prevents floods; irrigates luxuriant, year-round farmland across Southern California and Arizona, including the magnificent Imperial Valley; gives clear water to metropolitan Los Angeles and San Diego; and generates electrical power for Las Vegas and most of southern California. The population and industry of the modern Southwest are its offspring. The Allied victory in World War II owed much to ships and aircraft built in factories powered by the Hoover Dam.

13   [The dam's] career as a symbol began even before it was finished, when Americans looked to it for reassurance that their nation, staggered by the Great Depression, could still achieve great things.

After Reading Strategy: Deciding Whether the Author's Goals Were Met

Earlier you read how determining the purpose of a reading is an important strategy before reading. Purpose also plays a role after reading a passage.

Authors have goals when they write, but sometimes, it's harder than it should be for readers to discover them. Other times it can be clear what the goals are when you start reading but less clear when you finish. As a result, it's important to take a minute to think about a reading when you finish to discover if you think the author's goals were met. In other words, **did the author accomplish communicating everything he or she wanted the readers to know?**

After you have finished a text, do a quick analysis of how well you think the author met the goals by asking yourself these questions:

1. Was the author's goal(s) for writing the text as clear at the end of the text as at the beginning?

2. If it wasn't, where do you think things got off track or where did things change? Where did you get lost?

3. What do you think the author could have done to meet the goal(s)?

Practice Activity: Deciding Whether the Author's Goals Were Met

Answer these questions about your experience with Academic Reading 2.

1. What do you think the author's intent was? To inform? To persuade? To entertain? Was it accomplished?

_____

2. Were there any other possible reasons that the author was writing? To stir emotion? To inspire? To teach? Do you think it was accomplished?

_____

_____

3. What does the reading include (or lack) in trying to achieve that purpose?

_____

_____

Practice Activity: Reading for the Big Picture

Circle the correct information about the reading.

1. Diverting the Colorado River _is / is not_ one of the greatest feats of engineering in history.

2. The pouring of concrete was _huge, but not tricky / tricky, but not huge / both huge and tricky._

3. Pouring concrete _was / was not_ the biggest problem the engineers faced.

4. The beginning of the process went _slowly / quickly._

5. It is _easy / not easy_ to count all the benefits of Hoover Dam.

6. Americans saw the Hoover Dam as a symbol of reassurance that the country could do great things _before / during / after_ the Great Depression.

Summarizing What You Have Read

Summarize the main points of the original without re-using too many words or phrases from the original.

1. Somehow the concrete had to be carried to the dam at great speed, because the mixture required at the Hoover Dam was unusually dry to ensure it would set properly.

   _____

   _____

   _____

2. Inspired by devices he had made for earlier dams, Crowe wove a web of five cableways high above the canyon floor.

   _____

   _____

   _____

3. A time-lapse movie of the dam in progress would show shapes rising one block at a time to form 230 towering columns, with the columns standing up against each other to form a thick wall between the canyon's cliffs.

   _____

   _____

   _____

Your Active Vocabulary in the Real World

Vocabulary is important. Some words are useful for your speaking or for your writing, but other words are useful for your reading or your listening. For each word, decide how you think you will probably need this word for your English. Put a check mark (✓) under the ways you think you are likely to need the word. It is possible to have a check mark in more than one column.

	YOUR VOCABULARY	I need to be able to use this word in WRITING.	I need to be able to use this word in SPEAKING.	I need to understand this word in READING.	I need to understand this word in LISTENING.
1.	enumerate				
2.	ponder				
3.	a concept				
4.	pave				
5.	or so				
6.	flow				
7.	flooded				
8.	collapse				
9.	an asteroid				
10.	ancient				

Rapid Vocabulary Review

From the three answers on the right, circle the one that best explains, is an example of, or combines with the vocabulary word on the left as it is used in this unit.

Vocabulary	Answers		
Synonyms			
1. dangle	bring	grab	hang
2. irrigate	add water	add air	add land
3. an impact	imagination	an effect	a tradition
4. haul	run	force	pull
5. commerce	business	benefit	element
6. generate	prove	create	process
7. ingenious	brilliant	dangerous	unintelligent
8. ancient	primary	similar	old
9. stream	small job	small amount	small river
10. a spot	a job	a place	a wish
11. flow	vanish	decide	move
12. a beaver	an animal	a plant	a person
Combinations and Associations			
13. ___ a goal	put	run	set
14. in a ___ area	desert	tree	very
15. hold in ___	place	site	location
16. ___ half a million	about	or so	as well
17. pour a ___	person	liquid	result
18. a loss ___ power	by	of	to
19. bring ___ a halt	by	since	to
20. stomp ___	at	with	on

Vocabulary Log

To increase your vocabulary knowledge, write a definition or translation for each vocabulary item. Then write an original phrase, sentence, or note that will help you remember the vocabulary item.

Vocabulary Item	Definition or Translation	Your Original Phrase, Sentence, or Note
1. release	to let go	She released the balloon.
2. eliminate		
3. irrigate		
4. turn out		
5. a feat		
6. invert		
7. concept		
8. or so		
9. gravel		
10. compress		
11. penetrate		
12. damage		
13. regime		
14. excavate		

Vocabulary Item	Definition or Translation	Your Original Phrase, Sentence, or Note
15. magnify		
16. harden		
17. a scaffold		
18. roughly		
19. supply		
20. play a trick		
21. at hand		
22. mud		
23. inhabit		
24. precise		
25. merely		

3 Linguistics: Communication

Linguistics is the study of language. There are many things linguists study, but there are two general parts of language that most people are familiar with: verbal and non-verbal communication. Verbal communication includes the words people use to communicate messages. Some linguists study word meanings and origins—where words came from. Non-verbal communication includes messages communicated without using any words. This unit addresses the myths associated with one word in particular and non-verbal communication in general.

Part 1: Myths about Words

Getting Started

Linguistics is the science of language and linguists' attempt to prove and disprove ideas and theories just as scientists in other fields do. Sometimes they try to figure out why one word has more than one meaning or why there are several words that all mean the same thing or have similar meanings. Answer these questions with a partner.

1. Can you think of any English words that are synonyms or have a similar meaning? For example, *windy* and *breezy* are similar. List any you can think of.

   _____

   _____

   _____

2. Are there any words in another language you know that have more than one meaning? Are there words that share meanings with another word? Teach them to your partner.

   _____

   _____

   _____

3. Do you think having more than one word to describe something is good or bad? Can you think of any benefits? Any drawbacks? Do you think this makes learning a second language easier or harder?

   _____

   _____

   _____

About Unit 3: Academic Reading 1

Academic Reading 1 is from a book titled *Word Myths: Debunking Linguistic Urban Legends*, a book used as a textbook or for readers interested in linguistics. The passage discusses the word *snow* and other words that may or may not mean the same thing. It explores the history of the word in relation to one culture, the Eskimos, and whether or not the number of words affects how people think.

Before Reading Strategy: Predicting

Making some predictions before you read a text is a beneficial and common pre-reading strategy. In some ways, it may seem similar to activating prior knowledge, but it's different. It's different because even if you don't know anything about the topic, you can predict what you might find in the reading just by looking for the right clues.

When you **predict,** you use the information you've been given, such as the title, to get some idea about the topic to prepare you for what you might read. For example, you know this is a unit on the discipline of linguistics, or language, so you can make some predictions about what the reading will be about just based on that information. If you look at the title of first reading, you can see that the reading is about a myth about a word. If you know what a myth is, that will already tell you a bit about what the author of this text is going to say or how the reading will be structured—to support the myth or to debunk it (prove it wrong).

You can also use the headings and any photos or figures as clues to help you predict what the content of the reading may be. In terms of vocabulary, what words do you think you might find that are related to language or myths?

Remember that it isn't important if your predictions are incorrect. What is important is that you spent time thinking about the topic and preparing to read.

Practice Activity: Predicting

Look at the title of Academic Reading 1 on page 63. Then answer the questions. Do not read Academic Reading 1 yet.

1. List six vocabulary items (words or phrases) that you predict you will find in a reading on this topic and with this title.

   _____   _____

   _____   _____

   _____   _____

2. Can you guess what the myth is about the word *snow?* What other predictions can you make about the content of the reading?

   _____

   _____

   _____

   _____

Vocabulary Strategy: Recognizing Parts of Speech

You can probably name the parts of speech and what they do (for example, a noun is a person, place, or thing), but do you always use this knowledge when encountering unknown vocabulary? **Recognizing a word's part of speech** will help you grow your vocabulary and improve your understanding when reading. Even if you don't know what a word means, starts with the part of speech. There are two important things to notice about a word:

1. the suffix

Suffixes can help you identify a word because they don't change the word's meaning. Instead they tell you the word's function. For example, the suffix *–tion* means the word is a noun (*replication, evaluation*). A word that ends in *–ate* is usually a verb (*replicate, evaluate*). For more on word parts, see Appendix C.

2. the context (the words before and after it)

The words before or after an unknown word can also help determine its part of speech and its meaning. For example, nouns are often preceded by articles (*a, an, the*). If there is a word between an article and a noun, it is probably an adjective. Sometimes nouns have an *–s* ending (indicating they are plural). Remember that an *–s* ending can also be the present tense of a verb.

Don't confuse verb tense endings with other parts of speech. For example, is *running* a verb, an adjective, or a noun (gerund) in these sentences?

Running is a good way to stay in shape.
He was running to catch the bus when it started to rain.
The running tap water led to the flood in the bathroom.

Practice Activity: Recognizing Parts of Speech

Look at these suffixes. Write a word that includes each suffix. What part of speech is each? The first one has been done for you as an example.

1. *–ify*   verb _____
            simplify _____

2. *–y*   _____
            _____

3. *–ness* _____
            _____

4. *–ly*   _____
            _____

5. *–ment* _____
            _____

6. *–ed*   _____
            _____

7. *–ful*   _____
            _____

8. *–ion*   _____
            _____

9. *–ic*   _____
            _____

10. *–al*   _____
            _____

Vocabulary Power

There are a number of terms and phrases in this reading that you may encounter in other academic settings. Add at least five vocabulary items to your vocabulary notebook or log.

Match the words in bold from the reading on the left with a definition on the right.

_____ 1. Underlying this myth is the **assumption** that this, if true, is somehow significant.

_____ 2. Linguistic determinism holds that language determines how we think, that how we classify and categorize concepts into words, defines our **outlook** on the world.

_____ 3. Stephen Pinker summarized the debunking in his best-selling book *The Language Instinct,* . . . . Still, the myth **persists**.

_____ 4. Whorf argued that Eskimos were capable of greater understanding of arctic weather patterns because they had at their **disposal** a larger number of words with which to think about the subject.

_____ 5. To an Eskimo, this all-inclusive word would be almost unthinkable; he would say that falling snow, slushy snow, and so on, are sensuously and operationally different, different things to **contend with**; he uses different words for them and for other kinds of snow.

_____ 6. The fact that Yup'ik and Inuit languages have a large number of lexemes for snow is **trivial** and unremarkable.

_____ 7. The equivalent may not be a single word, but English is as equally **adept** at expressing distinctions in types of snow as Inuit or Yup'ik.

_____ 8. The fact that there is a large number of words for a thing does not indicate anything other than the fact that one has stumbled into the specialized **jargon** of some field.

a. special vocabulary

b. fight against

c. belief

d. unimportant

e. viewpoint

f. able, skillful

g. availability

h. continues

Academic Reading 1

Now, read the passage.

The Myth about the Word *Snow*

1   The myth is that Eskimos have a large number (50, 100, 500, it varies in the telling) of words for snow.** Underlying this myth is the assumption that this, if true, is somehow significant. Part of this assumption is the belief that the number of words for something reflects its sociological importance and affects how one thinks. Another part of the assumption is the common theme in urban legends that foreign cultures are strange and different, such as Eskimos kiss by rubbing noses. If they do this, it would seem strange for them not to have odd linguistic customs. Of course, all these beliefs about arctic cultures are false, including the one about language.

2   But where did this myth start? It began much like a snowball rolling downhill, becoming larger and larger until it was too big to stop. In 1911, anthropologist Franz Boas (*The Handbook of North American Indians, Vol. 1*) made casual reference to the "fact" that Eskimos had four root words for snow. Boas made the comment in the context of the observation that so-called "primitive" languages were no such thing. Instead, they were every bit as complex and rich as the languages of industrialized Western nations.

3   The next person in the chain of events leading to the myth was linguist Benjamin Lee Whorf. One of Whorf's major contributions to the field of linguistics was Sapir-Whorf Hypothesis, named for Whorf and his teacher Edward Sapir. The hypothesis had two main component principles, linguistic determination and linguistic relativity. Linguistic determinism holds that language determines how we think, that how we classify and categorize concepts into words defines our outlook on the world. Linguistic relativity holds that verbal distinctions in one language are not necessarily found in others. Germans or Eskimos, for example, think differently from English speakers because their language is different.

**David Wilton, the author of *Word Myths*, is not the first to debunk this myth. According to him, "Laura Martin was the first [to do this] in 'Eskimo Words for Snow' (*American Anthropologist*, Vol. 88, No. 2, June 1986). Geoffrey Pullum published a more popular debunking in *The Great Eskimo Vocabulary Hoax* (University of Chicago Press, 1991). Stephen Pinker summarized the debunking in his best-selling book *The Language Instinct* (William Morrow, 1994). Still, the myth persists."

4   In a 1940 article (published in *Technology Review* by the Massachusetts Institute of Technology), Whorf argued that the number of Eskimo words for snow was evidence of linguistic determination. Whereas English only had one word for snow, Eskimo had seven; Whorf argued that Eskimos were capable of greater understanding of arctic weather patterns because they had at their disposal a larger number of words with which to think about the subject. Whorf wrote:

> We have the same word for falling snow, snow on the ground, snow packed hard like ice, slushy snow, wind-driven flying snow— whatever the situation may be. To an Eskimo, this all-inclusive word would be almost unthinkable; he would say that falling snow, slushy snow, and so on, are sensuously and operationally different, different things to contend with; he uses different words for them and for other kinds of snow.

5   . . . The flaw is that Whorf has taken an overly simplistic view of the English language, which has many different words for *snow*. Falling snow can be *snow, flurries,* or *sleet.* Slushy snow is, obviously, *slush.* Wind-blown, flying snow is a *blizzard.* Other words include *frost, flakes, powder, drift,* and *avalanche,* to name a few. . . .

6   But in its day, Whorf's arguments were taken more seriously and were repeated again and again. In this repetition, the number of Eskimo words for snow increases. Boas had four. Whorf had seven. Soon there were a dozen, then fifty, then 100, then 200 words. And so on. So, how many Eskimo words for snow are there? . . .

7   So, depending on how you define "word," there can be anything from a handful to dozens of Eskimo words for snow (but not 500). . . . The Eskimo languages of Yup'ik and Inuit do not have a large number of "words" for snow, as English speakers understand the term. But they do have a very sophisticated linguistic capability for distinguishing between different types of snow. So at its core, the myth is basically true even if the details are misleading. But is this significant?

8   The answer is an unqualified NO. The fact that Yup'ik and Inuit languages have a large number of lexemes for snow is trivial and unremarkable. For each of the Inuit words listed, there is a fairly simple English language equivalent, such as *pack ice.* The equivalent may not be a single word, but English is as equally adept at expressing distinctions in types of snow as Inuit or Yup'ik.

9   Going beyond snow, every specialty field has a large vocabulary for items that are important to that field. . . . The fact that there is a large number of words for a thing does not indicate anything other than the fact that one has stumbled into the specialized jargon of some field.

10   The conclusion is that yes, even though the details are exaggerated and confused, the legend about Eskimo words for snow is basically true. The Native Americans of the far north have a sophisticated way to express winter weather conditions. But so what? Skiers in the Pocono Mountains do as well. This fact is utterly unremarkable. If the Yup'ik and Inuit peoples did not have a large number of ways to express different types of arctic weather conditions, we should be surprised.

FYI: Understanding Footnotes, Part 2

Bibliographic footnotes were discussed on page 10. There is another type of footnote common in academic reading that is not bibliographic. Usually these notes appear at the bottom of the page like bibliographic footnotes, but occasionally they appear at the end of the chapter or at the end of the book and are called endnotes.

These non-bibliographic footnotes include information that the author wants to include for readers but does not think is essential to understanding the reading. The type of information in these types of footnotes varies. The one on page 63, for example, provides information about one of the author's claims. In Unit 4, you will see many other types of **informational footnotes**. Because the information is not included in the reading per se, you don't need to read them. However, when studying, keep in mind that some professors test on the material included in the footnotes and that this information may be useful in research for a paper or discussion.

After Reading Strategy: Evaluating the Reading Experience

When you finish an academic reading or a reading on a topic that is new or challenging to you, it's important to reflect on and evaluate the strategies you employed to understand the reading. Research on what good readers do shows that this step is an important one in improving reading skills. This is because when readers understand which strategies work better for them with certain types of texts, they become more efficient readers over-all. You will have a chance to review all the strategies in Unit 6.

This stategy also helps you get into the practice of thinking about the reading process afterward. Did you end up skimming? Did you enjoy it? Did you learn something?

After you have completed an academic reading, do a quick analysis of the experience by asking yourself these questions:

1. How much of this reading did I understand?
    100%? 50%? Very little?

2. Which parts of the text were the easiest to understand? Why?

3. Which parts of the text were the hardest to understand? Why?

4. Did I use any strategies **before, during,** or **after** I read to help me understand? If so, which ones?

5. Did I like this?

6. What did I learn?

Practice Activity: Evaluating the Reading Experience

Answer these questions about your experience with Academic Reading 1.

1. How much of this reading did I understand?

   _____

2. Which parts of the text were the easiest to understand? Why?

   _____

3. Which parts of the text were the hardest to understand? Why?

   _____

4. Which **before, during,** or **after** reading strategies did I use to help me understand?

   _____

   _____

Practice Activity: Reading for the Big Picture

Write T if the statement is true or F if the statement is false.

1. _____ Eskimos have a large number of words that mean "snow."

2. _____ The myth about the word *snow* started small and grew larger over time.

3. _____ Whorf's view of the English language was too simplistic.

4. _____ Every field has a large vocabulary of items that are special to it.

5. _____ The legend about Eskimo words to describe snow is simply not true.

Summarizing What You Have Read

Summarize the main points of the original without re-using too many words or phrases from the original.

1. Linguistic determinism holds that language determines how we think, that how we classify and categorize concepts into words defines our outlook on the world.

   _____

   _____

   _____

2. . . . Whorf argued that Eskimos were capable of greater understanding of arctic weather patterns because they had at their disposal a larger number of words with which to think about the subject.

   _____

   _____

   _____

3. The fact that there is a large number of words for a thing does not indicate anything other than the fact that one has stumbled into the specialized jargon of some field.

   _____

   _____

   _____

Part 2: Non-Verbal Communication

Getting Started

Non-verbal communication can accompany words, but it can also be used without any words at all. Most non-verbal messages are communicated visually. In many cases, it is just as powerful as using words. Answer these questions with a partner.

1. What are some ways that people communicate without using words?

   _____

   _____

   _____

   _____

2. When might non-verbal communication be more appropriate than a verbal message? In what situations would you use non-verbal communication or a gesture to accompany a verbal message?

   _____

   _____

   _____

   _____

3. People in the United States often wave as a non-verbal message to mean *hello* or *goodbye*. What is one message that people in your native culture often share non-verbally?

   _____

   _____

   _____

   _____

About Unit 3: Academic Reading 2

Academic Reading 2 is titled *The Basics of Non-Verbal Communication* and comes from a textbook used in a Linguistics or Introduction to Language course (*Topics in Language and Culture*). Its purpose is to inform readers about important aspects of non-verbal communication.

Before Reading Strategy: Previewing Text Patterns

One common pre-reading strategy, especially with textbook readings, is to look at the text pattern. It is a good idea to be familiar with and identify the text pattern being used before beginning the reading. Previewing the text pattern is a good strategy if the topic is one that you aren't familiar with. It is similar in some ways to predicting. The pattern or structure of the text—particularly academic, non-fiction texts—can provide a sense of the important parts of the material before you start reading and can help you get a head-start on understanding the main ideas. It also makes it easier to follow the argument or flow of the passage. To preview:

1. Read the title and all of the subheadings.
2. Read any material that stands out, such as text in lists or text that is in **boldface** or *italic* type. Look for words that indicate a pattern, such as numbers: *Non-verbal communication consists of three systems: proxemics, kinesics, and paralanguage.*
3. Look for other phrasing that might give you information about the reading, such as language to indicate the text is going to compare and contrast different items, such as *compared to, in contrast to,* or *a comparison.* A **cause-and-effect text** might include phrases such as *as a result of* or *a consequence of.* A **process or chronological text** might include words such as *first, then, next, after, when,* or *finally.*

Transition words or phrases such as *however* and *therefore* are also useful in showing relationships between and among ideas.

Practice Activity: Previewing Text Patterns

1. Look at Academic Reading 2 on pages 74–78. List the subheadings.

   _____   _____

   _____   _____

   _____

2. You know from the strategy box that the reading includes a sentence that mentions three types of non-verbal communication. The three types are given in boldface in the reading. If the reading were going to focus on these three types of communication, you would find headings for all three of them in the reading. Look at your list in #1. Are all of them listed? If not, which ones are mentioned? What does that tell you about the focus of the reading?

   _____

   _____

3. Skim the reading for words that are in boldface or italic type. List them. What do they indicate about the focus of the reading?

   _____

   _____

   _____

4. Look at the first sentence in Paragraph 3. What does it indicate will be the focus of this section? Is there specific language that tells you where that section ends?

   _____

   _____

5. Based on your preview of the reading, do you think the reading is more likely to be comparing and contrasting items, describing a process, or showing a cause-effect relationship? Explain your answer.

   _____

   _____

   _____

abc

Vocabulary Strategy: Identifying Coordinating Conjunctions and Similar Words

Coordinating conjunctions are words that connect two related ideas. The conjunction can show the reader how words, sentences, phrases, or clauses are important to each other. There are seven coordinating conjunctions: *for, and, nor, but, or, yet, so.* To remember these, learn FANBOYS.

Each conjunction has a meaning that tells the reader how the words before it are related to the words after it.

for: gives a reason
and: adds a similar and equal idea
nor: connects two negative but equal ideas
but: adds a different or opposite idea
or: joins two equal ideas or alternatives
yet: offers an opposite idea
so: gives a result or consequence

English has several similar, **yet** not exact, words to describe wind.
You know how to read English well, **but** you do not know how to read German.
Do you prefer reading English *or* writing English?

Conjunctions also have other words or phrases that can offer similar meanings. Knowing these words is helpful when paraphrasing or when trying to comprehend a reading.

For example, other words for *and* are: **also, besides, furthermore, too, in addition,** or **moreover.**

Practice Activity: Identifying Coordinating Conjunctions and Similar Words

A. List another word for each of these conjunctions.

    1. *but* _____   3. *yet* _____

    2. *or* _____   4. *so* _____

B. What word could be used to connect two parts of the sentence to make it clear for the reader?

Gestures like those mentioned so far are not conventionalized, _____ individuals may not agree on the "proper" way to describe an accident or display lack of trust.

Vocabulary Power

There are a number of terms and phrases in this reading that you may encounter in other academic settings. Add at least five vocabulary items to your vocabulary notebook or log.

Match the words in bold from the reading on the left with a definition on the right.

_____ 1. Gestures like those mentioned so far are not conventionalized; individuals may not agree on the "proper" way to describe an accident or **display** lack of trust.

_____ 2. Their reason for existence may in fact be to **substitute** for speech (often taboo speech).

_____ 3. Their reason for existence may in fact be to substitute for speech (often **taboo** speech).

_____ 4. Cultures differ greatly in their use of **emblems**; this can have both amusing, inconsequential results and quite serious results for business and diplomacy.

_____ 5. Cultures differ greatly in their use of emblems; this can have both amusing, **inconsequential** results and quite serious results for business and diplomacy.

_____ 6. Cultures differ on **appropriacy** of eye contact.

_____ 7. Many Asian, Caribbean, and African cultures think direct or lengthy eye contact is **rude** or aggressive.

_____ 8. A lot of meaning is **conveyed** between students and teachers through posture, facial expression, and eye contact.

a. reveal

b. unimportant

c. replace

d. correctness

e. forbidden

f. impolite

g. communicated

h. signs

Academic Reading 2

Now, read the passage.

The Basics of Non-Verbal Communication

1   Non-verbal communication can emphasize, contradict, or substitute for verbal behavior. Non-verbal communication consists of three systems: proxemics, kinesics, and paralanguage. **Proxemics** is the study of how space is used to communicate. **Kinesics** is the study of body motion; it covers the areas of gestures, posture, touching, facial expressions, and eye contact. **Paralanguage** is concerned with the use of the voice during speech—pitch, loudness, and rate of speech, among other things.

2   While non-verbal communication varies to a certain degree within nationalities and groups (according to age, gender, and ethnicity), it is possible to make some general observations and contrasts. Because of globalization and increased mobility of populations, few countries have one culture. . . . Let's take a closer look at kinesics.

Kinesics: Motion and Communication

Gestures

3   Speakers use gestures for several different reasons. Gestures may help the speaker remember a word or help the speaker keep an idea "at hand," so to speak. Gestures may also play a role in conversation by allowing the listener to give feedback silently. They may be useful in a conversation to indicate the place and time something happened. Gestures may fill in for a word. They may indicate an entire speech act, such as a simple shrug or the southern Italian *hand purse*, which indicates *Why?* (Kendon, 1997).

4   *Gesture* is a broad word that has been used for many distinct activities. McNeill (1992) presents what he calls "Kendon's continuum" of gestures. At one end is *gesticulation,* which is always accompanied by speech; gesticulation indeed helps form

speech. Someone may talk about an accident and may show, simultaneous with speech, the movements of the cars involved. What McNeill calls *language-like gestures* are those that substitute for words in a sentence. Someone may say, "He's a little . . . " and finish the sentence with a movement of the hand, palm down, wrist slightly rotated back and forth, to indicate disapproval, lack of trust, or shakiness. Gestures like those mentioned so far are not conventionalized; individuals may not agree on the "proper" way to describe an accident or display lack of trust. *Pantomimes* too lack convention-alization, for the most part. They are characterized by a complete lack of speech. One roommate may tell another who is talking on the phone through pantomime that she's going to go out and come back. There might be more agreement among members of the culture about the best way to accomplish this than the best way to describe an accident.

5   *Emblems* are the sort of gestures that we usually mean when we use the word *gesture*. They have conventional meanings within the culture and are not accompanied by speech. Their reason for existence may

in fact be to substitute for speech (often taboo speech). Another characteristic of emblems is that there is agreement on their form. The *OK* sign cannot be made with the thumb and the third finger; instead, it is made with the thumb and index finger forming a circle. It's not insulting to hold up the ring finger by itself. Emblems include the head toss and the thumb held to the nose. Another emblem is the horn sign using the hand that the University of Texas uses as a rallying symbol and that in southern Italy is considered impolite.

6   The end of this continuum is occupied by sign languages. These are very different from the other gestures, being complete, well-formed, auto-nomous languages.

Cultural Differences in Emblems

7   Cultures differ greatly in their use of emblems; this can have both amusing, inconsequential results and quite serious results for business and diplomacy. There have been several famous examples of U.S. politicians unintentionally insulting large crowds by using American gestures. Richard Nixon, during a South American trip as Vice President, flashed the *OK* sign with both hands, not knowing it was an obscene,

insulting gesture to his audience. They booed. President George H. W. Bush made the *V for Victory* sign as he rode in a limousine through a crowd of Australians. The trouble was his palm was facing him, not the crowd. This is an obscene gesture in Australia (and England), comparable to one made with one middle finger in the United States. Similarly, the "thumbs up" gesture is considered obscene in many countries.

8   Most cultures have set routines for greeting others. In North America, handshakes are common. The best handshake is considered to be a firm one that does not last too long and is accompanied by looking into the other person's eyes. Both handshakes and eye contact differ significantly in other parts of the world, however. A handshake in the Arab world may not be as firm as one between two North Americans, because a firm grip is considered aggressive. In Islamic countries, men and women are generally not allowed to shake hands. In Japan and Korea, direct eye contact when greeting (or at other times) may be considered disrespectful. In South America, a handshake may be accompanied by a hug and a pat on the back. Generally, North Americans shake hands at first meeting but may not shake hands with friends. The French

shake hands much more frequently than North Americans do. Something as simple as a handshake, then, turns out to be quite complex.

9   Not everyone shakes hands. In India and Thailand, the same gesture is used for greeting. The Indians call it a *namaste*, and the Thais call it a *wai*. It consists of putting the hands together in a prayer position, chest high. The gesture is frequently accompanied by a slight bow. The *salaam* is used by more traditional members of the older generation in the Middle East. The right hand is moved from the heart to the forehead and upward and outward.

10   Farewell gestures also differ. The American *goodbye* wave looks like the European and Latin American "no" gesture. In much of Europe, *goodbye* is also a wave, but the arm is extended with the palm down, not out. The hand moves at the wrist. This gesture looks quite a bit like the Japanese gesture for *come here*. The Greeks and Italians wave *goodbye* in a gesture that is familiar to Americans as *come here*— arm out, palm up, fingers curled back and forth.

11   In North America, nodding the head up and down generally means *yes* and shaking the head back and forth means *no*. Traditionally, in southeastern

Europe (the former Yugoslavia, Bulgaria, Greece, Turkey), Iran, and parts of India, the opposite was true. Throwing the head back in Greece and southern Italy may mean *no* (but in Germany may indicate that someone wants you to come closer). In parts of India, the head toss backward means *yes*.

Posture

12   The way we hold our bodies is often synchronized with the way we speak. We use gestures and lean closer to our conversation partner to make points. We change our facial expressions. We often synchronize our posture with other people as a sign of our involvement in (but not necessarily agreement with) the conversation. Posture lets people know we are interested in and following the conversation.

13   Cultures differ in their rules for carrying the body and maintaining it at rest. The Japanese and Koreans, for example, have traditionally sat on cushions on the floor while Europeans have sat on chairs. There are rules for polite sitting on the floor and polite sitting in chairs. When sitting on the floor in a formal situation in Japan or Korea, the feet are tucked under the buttocks so that the person is sitting on the heels of the feet. When sitting formally in chairs, Japanese men and women, as is true in the United States and many other countries, cross their legs differently, and in very formal situations should not cross them at all. Around the world, it is very common to see people waiting or resting in a squatting position, with their arms resting on their knees. Such a position is less frequently seen in the United States.

Eye Contact

14   Cultures differ on the appropriacy of eye contact. North American, British, Eastern European, and Saudi Arabian cultures favor eye contact. Arabs may be uncomfortable with a peripheral conversation such as one in which two people walk along side by side talking and may prefer to look at their conversational partners. Many Asian, Caribbean, and African cultures think direct or lengthy eye contact is rude or aggressive.

15   Non-verbal communication is an important element in classrooms. A lot of meaning is conveyed between students and teachers through posture, facial expression, and eye contact (Neill, 1991). Intercultural mis-understandings can arise in classrooms

when the cultures of students and the teacher disagree on the meanings of gestures, facial expressions, and eye contact. People new to teaching students from other cultures often interpret widespread nodding in the class as understanding, while the students may be indicating that they are paying attention. Common U.S. teacher behavior such as sitting on the teacher's desk can be seen by other cultures as inappropriate.

References

Kendon, Adam. (1997). "Gesture." *Annual Review of Anthropology, 26,* 109–128.

McNeil, David. (1992). *Hand and mind: What gestures reveal about thought.* Chicago: University of Chicago Press.

Neill, Sean. (1991). *Classroom nonverbal communication.* London: Routledge.

FYI: Understanding In-Text Citations and Bibliographic/Reference Entries

In some texts, in-text citations appear instead of bibliographic footnotes. See examples in Academic Reading 2 like this: (Kendon, 1997). The citation in parentheses provides the name(s) of author(s) and year of publication. It only includes this brief information because the rest of the publication information appears at the end of the article or book in the Bibliography, list of Works Cited, or list of References, depending on the style (APA, MLA).

The entry usually includes the author(s), the title, the publisher, and year of publication, as shown at the end of Academic Reading 2. If it's a book, the location of the publisher is also listed. If it's a magazine or journal article, the name of the publication is included with the volume number and/or issue number and page number.

If it's an online article, the name of the website and the URL are usually included.

After Reading Strategy: Drawing Conclusions

Often writers will directly state what they want you to know. They will tell you the conclusions to be drawn from the facts and examples they used. Think of these as **parting shots** or ideas that the author wants you take away from the reading. However, sometimes the conclusion is left unstated, and readers are expected to draw their own conclusions from the evidence presented.

1. If a paragraph or section doesn't end with a stated conclusion, ask yourself questions such as, *What is the importance of this? What do these examples mean about the topic? What did the author want me to know the most about this topic? Why did the writer choose to tell me these things?*

2. It may be helpful to re-read topic sentences in the final paragraphs or the introduction of a section. The writer may have stated the purpose of the passage in these sections.

3. If you can't determine a conclusion immediately, continue reading. Perhaps you will be able to draw a conclusion after a few more paragraphs. However, if that doesn't help, it's possible that you haven't totally understood what you have read. Check unfamiliar words in a dictionary, or talk with a classmate about the meaning of the passage.

4. Be careful, of course, not to draw conclusions that are not supported with evidence in the text. You must be able to state not only what you think the passage implies, but also why you think so.

Practice Activity: Drawing Conclusions from the Reading

Answer these questions about the reading.

1. Which places in the reading seem to be offering some conclusions or "parting shots"—things you should take away from the reading?

   _____

   _____

   _____

   _____

2. What are the things that you think the authors wanted you to know the most about this topic? How do you know?

_____

_____

_____

_____

3. Write a two-sentence conclusion of the importance of this reading. Compare your conclusions with a partner.

_____

_____

_____

_____

Practice Activity: Reading for the Big Picture

Choose the best answer to each question.

1. What is the main idea of the passage?

   a. There are three main systems of non-verbal communication.

   b. Different cultures view aspects of motion and communication in different ways.

   c. Some theorists argue that non-verbal communication depends on culture.

   d. There are cultural rules for the way people show their emotions.

2. Which components of non-verbal communication are included in kinesics? Choose all that are correct.

   a. study of how space is used   e. posture

   b. how voice is used   f. facial expressions

   c. gestures   g. rate of speech

   d. nationality

Summarizing What You Have Read

Summarize the main points of the original without re-using too many words or phrases from the original.

1. While non-verbal communication varies to a certain degree within nationalities and groups (according to age, gender, and ethnicity), it is possible to make some general observations and contrasts.

_____

_____

_____

2. Cultures differ greatly in their use of emblems; this can have both amusing, inconsequential results and quite serious results for business and diplomacy.

_____

_____

_____

3. We often synchronize our posture with other people as a sign of our involvement in (but not necessarily agreement with) the conversation.

_____

_____

_____

Your Active Vocabulary in the Real World

Vocabulary is important. Some words are useful for your speaking or for your writing, but other words are useful for your reading or your listening. For each word, decide how you think you will probably need this word for your English. Put a check mark (✓) under the ways you think you are likely to need the word. It is possible to have a check mark in more than one column.

	YOUR VOCABULARY	I need to be able to use this word in WRITING.	I need to be able to use this word in SPEAKING.	I need to understand this word in READING.	I need to understand this word in LISTENING.
1.	the rate				
2.	gender				
3.	an avalanche				
4.	flaw				
5.	and so on				
6.	jargon				
7.	utterly				
8.	slush				
9.	proper				
10.	gesture				

Rapid Vocabulary Review

From the three answers on the right, circle the one that best explains, is an example of, or combines with the vocabulary word on the left as it is used in this unit.

Vocabulary	Answers		
Synonyms			
1. significant	brief	important	minority
2. classify	categorize	reject	ignore
3. obscene	minimum	positive	crude
4. a flaw	a defect	a decade	a definition
5. sophisticated	mental	odd	advanced
6. boo	disapprove	unusual	abnormal
7. favor	complain	prefer	tighten
8. conventional	unique	global	traditional
9. routine	military	percent	pattern
10. proper	appropriate	major	lower
11. contradict	create	disagree	emerge
12. amusing	funny	isolated	maximum
Combinations and Associations			
13. ___ contact	coin	eye	voice
14. a ___ handshake	green	loud	firm
15. convey ___	reality	meaning	intelligence
16. a chain of ___	events	handshakes	areas
17. substitute ___	at	for	to
18. index ___	finger	book	person
19. and ___ on	by	so	then
20. ___ a role in	stand	run	play

Vocabulary Log

To increase your vocabulary knowledge, write a definition or translation for each vocabulary item. Then write an original phrase, sentence, or note that will help you remember the vocabulary item.

Vocabulary Item	Definition or Translation	Your Original Phrase, Sentence, or Note
1. hypothesis	guess	His research hypothesis was . . .
2. posture		
3. according to		
4. play a role (in)		
5. broad		
6. palm		
7. slightly		
8. accompanied by		
9. insult		
10. grip		
11. disrespectful		
12. gesture		
13. lean (v.)		
14. cushions		

Vocabulary Item	Definition or Translation	Your Original Phrase, Sentence, or Note
15. primitive		
16. myth		
17. a legend		
18. evidence		
19. blizzard		
20. interpret		
21. exaggerate		
22. turn out (to be)		
23. utterly		
24. debunk		
25. continuum		

4 Fine Arts: Art Appreciation

History is the study of the past and its effects on other events. Art history is the study of artwork and its role in the discipline and in the world. Art historians sometimes study the styles or the features of art created at certain times. Some events that happened in the art world are interesting to everyone, not just art historians. The readings in this unit are interesting in that one details a theft that surprised the art world and the other discusses an artist and the choices he made. Both illustrate the impact of art on the world.

Part 1: The Value of Art

Getting Started

The Isabella Stewart Gardner Museum is in Boston, Massachusetts. Isabella was an American art collector. She used money she inherited to buy many important pieces of art. She and her husband wanted a place to show their art. In 1903, she opened the museum, and it is home to more than 2,500 pieces of art, including many pieces by famous artists. In 1990, thieves broke into the museum and stole many well-known pieces from famous artists like Vermeer and Rembrandt. Answer these questions with a partner.

1. Name some well-known artists you are familiar with. Discuss their work.

   _____

   _____

   _____

2. Art is sometimes sold for hundreds of thousands of dollars (or more). How much do you think art is worth?

   _____

   _____

   _____

3. Imagine you were wealthy enough to be an art collector. What kinds of art would you collect for your own museum? Why?

   _____

   _____

   _____

   _____

About Unit 4: Academic Reading 1

Academic Reading 1 is from a book titled *The Gardner Heist.* The reading is similar to what you may read in a history or art history course. The passage discusses the famous theft at the Gardner Museum—one of the biggest unsolved crimes in history—and describes some of the pieces that were stolen. Its purpose is to address the price of art and discuss why people steal art.

Before Reading Strategy: Using SQ3R—Survey and Question

Before reading an academic passage, it is helpful to know the SQ3R method. It's been an effective reading strategy for many academic readers when all five steps are done consistently. The first two steps are taught here.

The SQ3R reading strategy is designed to help you read effectively so you can improve comprehension, write stronger papers, and perform better on tests about texts you have read. The first two letters in the SQ3R reading strategy stand for **Survey** and **Question,** and they should be done <u>before</u> you read.

Survey

Surveying helps you develop a broad overview of the reading. There are several parts of the reading you should survey before you read in-depth. This strategy is similar to skimming (see Unit 1). By noticing these parts, you are recognizing important features and can form questions about the content:

- title
- headings and subheadings
- illustrations, figures, or photos
- review questions
- objectives
- first paragraph
- last paragraph
- summary

Question

After you have completed a survey, you should focus on **questions**—those you write yourself or those provided by the author or your teacher.

- Convert the title, headings, and subheadings into questions.

- Read any review questions provided in the text or by your instructor.

- Create questions from the objectives given in the textbook.

- Think about questions that come to mind after you skim the first and last paragraphs.

- Ask yourself questions about what your instructor wants you to learn.

- Ask yourself what you already know about the topic.

- Ask yourself questions about what you hope to learn.

Leave room in your notebook for annotations to answer the questions later. Completing the Survey and Question steps before you read will strengthen your comprehension. It will also help you prepare for future readings. For example, in art appreciation or art history courses, you may read biographies of artists or critical reviews of artwork.

Practice Activity: Using SQ3R—Survey and Question

Survey Academic Reading 1, and write questions using the techniques listed. Then answer the three questions given. A question has been done for you as an example.

1. Title: _What is the real value of art?_____

2. Heading 1: _____

3. Heading 2: _____

4. Question from introductory paragraph: _____

5. Question from concluding paragraph: _____

6. What do I know about this topic? _____

7. What do I need to learn about this topic? _____

8. What does my instructor want me to learn by reading this?

   _____

During Reading Strategy: Using SQ3R—Read

The third letter in the SQ3R reading strategy stands for the first of the 3Rs, **Read.** Read does <u>not</u> mean that you will simply read the text passively. You will instead read actively. Reading actively requires being engaged with the text, including:

Read

1. Look for answers to the questions you raised during the Survey and Question phases. Annotate as you read.

2. Answer the questions you created from the title, headings, and sub-headings.

3. Notice pictures, charts, graphs, or other illustrations, and read the captions.

4. Read slowly when you encounter new or challenging information.

5. Read carefully when you see words or phrases in boldface or italic type or those called out in the margins. Make a list of new words or phrases, and add them to your vocabulary log.

A careful, thorough reading will not only help you understand the main idea and details but will also help you concentrate on vocabulary. Thinking about the information as you read will help you determine the author's purpose and draw conclusions to deepen your understanding of the text.

Practice Activity: Using SQ3R—Read

As you read, answer the questions you wrote on page 89. Then answer these questions with a partner.

1. Did you find answers to your questions? _____

2. What vocabulary words or phrases did you notice?

   _____

   _____

   _____

3. Were there any illustrations or photos? What did they show? Why do you think they were included?

   _____

   _____

   _____

4. Were there any parts of the reading you found challenging or that you read more slowly? Did you eventually understand those sections of the reading?

   _____

   _____

   _____

5. Were there any parts of the reading you re-read to improve your understanding?

   _____

   _____

   _____

Vocabulary Power

There are a number of terms and phrases in this reading that you may encounter in other academic settings. Add at least five vocabulary items to your vocabulary notebook or log.

Match the words in bold from the reading on the left with a definition on the right.

_____ 1. When the Metropolitan Museum of Art bought Rembrandt's *Aristotle Contemplating the Bust of Homer* in 1961, many thought the museum had been **conned**.

_____ 2. Now people buy art for profit, purchasing paintings like a **broker** arbitrages Coca-Cola or Microsoft stock.

_____ 3. . . . and there seemed no doubt that the thieves knew that the Gardner works were highly valuable **commodities**.

_____ 4. Museums **neglect** security for all kinds of reasons.

_____ 5. Private institutions have come to rely entirely on the **fickle** ways of fund-raising.

_____ 6. A full **roster** of guards can eat up half of a museum's operating budget and that doesn't include infrastructure costs such as video cameras, motion detectors, and electronic keys.

_____ 7. A full roster of guards can eat up half of a museum's operating budget and that doesn't include **infrastructure** costs such as video cameras, motion detectors, and electronic keys.

_____ 8. Museums often think that they're protected by that art **mystique**—but it's often the reverse that's true.

a. basic things

b. not pay attention to

c. list

d. items bought and sold

e. cheated

f. changeable

g. fascination

h. agent

Academic Reading 1

Now, read the passage.

The Real Value of Art

1   Art wasn't always so expensive. The boom began in the 1960s, and since then prices have taken off at irrationally exuberant levels, with the values of some well-known artists jumping more than 1,000 percent. The appreciation is far greater than other traded commodities, be it stocks or real estate or oil, and while the market has had some dips over the years, the frenzy seems to always top itself. When the Metropolitan Museum of Art bought Rembrandt's *Aristotle Contemplating the Bust of Homer* in 1961, many thought the museum had been conned. The $2.3 million price tag was more than twice the previous auction record, and *Time* magazine, which ran the painting on its cover that week, noted that "the only fitting motto is: 'Let the buyer beware.'" But the market continued its upward spiral. The record for the most expensive painting sold at an auction has been broken ten times since then; forty-five years to the month of the Rembrandt sale, Christie's* held an auction where almost every piece of art went for more than $2 million.

> **Christie's:** a well-known company that auctions or sells art and other expensive items, often from private collections

2   The engine behind the boom is partly the prices themselves. Many collectors buy big-time artists because they command big-time prices, with an increase in money, comes an increase in prestige. The art market also provides a curious twist on the usual supply-and-demand model because there is, in the end, an extremely limited supply. There is only one *Mona Lisa* [by da Vinci], one *Starry Night* [by Van Gogh], one *David* [by Michelangelo]. But the biggest driver might be the notion of art as an investment. In the past, people bought paintings and sculptures for beauty or status or merely to have an image of something important to them. Now people buy art for profit, purchasing paintings like a broker arbitrages Coca-Cola or Microsoft stock. Even some investment banks have gotten into the business, buying [Jackson] Pollocks low and selling them high. "We look at million-dollar deals every week and often buy $1 million to $2 million of art a week," Rhea Papinicolaou of the London Fine Art fund [says]. Her fund showed an average of 47 percent return on sales. She said, "If you have an excellent team of experts, are sitting on a lot of cash, and are prepared to hold art over a ten-year period, you can make substantial profits."

The Value of the Gardner Paintings

3   The estimated worth of the stolen Gardner paintings has shown the same meteoric rise as the rest of the market. When Gardner purchased the Vermeer [*The Concert*] in 1892, she paid 29,000 French francs, or about $6,000. A few years later, Gardner's friend Ralph Curtis wrote her from the Hague, "[Hofstede de Groote] says your *Concert* is now worth *easily* between hundred and fifty and two hundred thousand. . . . " This fact remained true for much of the next century—and there seems no doubt that the thieves knew that the Gardner works were highly valuable commodities. Six months before the theft, Christie's sold Manet's *The Rue Mosnier with Flags* for $26.4 million. The price more than doubled the record for a work by the artist, and the sale made headlines across the country. The auction record for a Rembrandt painting was set just a year before the robbery when *Portrait of a Bearded Man in a Red Coat* sold for about $10 million. And after the heist, some blamed the museum break-in squarely on the market itself. "The [Gardner] theft is the blue-collar side of the glittering system whereby art, through the '80s, was promoted in crass totems of excess capital," wrote one critic. "If one wanted a perfect example of how the crazed art market has come to work against American museums and their public, what happened in Boston last week would be it."

4   Whatever the case, the art market continues to skyrocket—and the notional value of the stolen Gardner art climbs along with it. When the FBI first announced the caper, they estimated the loss at $200 million; eight years later, the *Boston Herald* put the price at over $400 million, with the Vermeer at $238 million, *The Storm* [by Rembrandt] at $140 million, and the rest of the works in the many thousands. . . . Today, a few dealers say the stolen Gardner paintings could be worth as much as $600 million. . . .

5   When [thieves] hear the prices commanded by top paintings and sculptures—and realize how poorly secured they are—art theft becomes a given. A few years after a Leonardo da Vinci codex sold for a record-breaking $31 million, two men strolled into the Drumlanrig Castle in Scotland. They looked like regular tourists. They wore sensible shoes, thick coats, and baseball hats. Then, about halfway through the tour, one of the men threatened a docent with a knife, while the other pulled da Vinci's painting *Madonna with the Yarnwinder* from the wall. The men leaped out of a kitchen window and into a waiting VW Golf sedan. The heist took less than ten minutes—and the thieves disappeared with a four-by-six foot piece

of canvas valued at more than $200 million. With such a massive return on such little effort, one has to wonder—why do [thieves] steal anything else?

The Problem of Museum Security

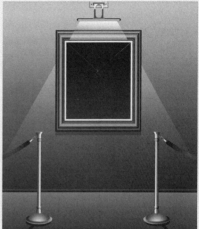

The Gardner Museum did not remove the displays of the stolen paintings. The frames were left in place.

6   Museums neglect security for all kinds of reasons. Lack of foresight, lack of imagination, lack of vigor, and even the world's most prestigious museums suffer from a lack of resources. Over the past few decades, governments have reduced or eliminated subsidies. Private institutions have come to rely entirely on the fickle ways of fund-raising. Budget problems have become so severe that many institutions have limited services or darkened galleries . . . .

7   At the same time, the cost of security is going up. A full roster of guards can eat up half of a museum's operating budget and that doesn't include infrastructure costs such as video cameras, motion detectors, and electronic keys. . . . Guards are often a weak point. Museums don't provide much in terms of training—usually just a week-long introductory session—and the salaries are painfully low. Most institutions just pay a dollar or two more than a burger-flipper at McDonald's. Guards also give the position short shrift, and the FBI estimates that more than 80 percent of all museum heists have an inside angle. A guard might provide a thief with a detailed description of the alarm system, or the night watchman will pocket something while working late one evening. . . .

8   The biggest problem was not the technology or the guards or even the alarms, but the fact that galleries didn't really believe they would ever get robbed: "Museums often think that they're protected by that art mystique, but it's often the reverse that's true. Thieves steal art because it's easy."

After Reading Strategy: Using SQ3R—Recite and Review

The final two Rs in the SQ3R reading strategy stand for **Recite** and **Review.** Recite and review are done after you finish reading.

Recite

- Ask yourself questions about what you read.

- Summarize the reading in your own words.

- Look at your notes, and read your answers to the questions.

- Say the vocabulary words and phrases, and take time to learn their definitions.

Do these actions aloud so that you are hearing and seeing the material simultaneously. By doing so, you are using two senses (sight and hearing) and are more likely to remember. To further develop the reciting of material, make notes.

Review

- After you recite, continue to read your answers to questions, and write new questions and answers in the margins.

- Make sure to answer questions about the main ideas.

- Draw conclusions about the topic.

- Try to recite or write answers from memory.

- Make guesses about any information that may be asked about later.

It helps to create an SQ3R chart or graph (see page 97) to help you organize all of the questions and answers during the Review stage. Put your questions in the left column and your answers in the right column. You can then study from this chart each day.

Completing the five steps of the SQ3R reading strategy will help you get to know the reading material well. If you do so, you will not have to "cram" for an exam or spend as much time re-reading later.

Practice Activity: Completing an SQ3R Chart

Complete the chart.

Questions or Annotations	Answers or Details
Questions from titles or headings	
Notes about pictures or illustrations	
Notes about my annotations	
Questions from the reading	
Questions from the reciting	
What are the main ideas?	
What conclusions can be drawn?	
What vocabulary items are important?	

Practice Activity: Reading for the Big Picture

Choose the best answer to each question.

1. What is the main idea of the passage?

   a. Art thefts happen because of high prices and little security.

   b. Art prices have increased at the same rate as art thefts.

   c. The Gardner theft took place because the art prices skyrocketed.

   d. The biggest problem with museum security is the technology.

2. What are the reasons that museums neglect security even though it increases the chances of theft? Choose all that are correct.

   a. guard salaries are too high to pay

   b. decreased budgets

   c. fund-raising replaces stolen art

   d. belief that museums won't be robbed

   e. belief that it's easy to steal

   f. poor technology

   g. government funding has decreased

Summarizing What You Have Read

Summarize the main points of the original without re-using too many words or phrases from the original.

1. The art market also provides a curious twist on the usual supply-and-demand model because there is, in the end, an extremely limited supply.

   _____

   _____

   _____

2. Whatever the case, the art market continues to skyrocket—and the notional value of the stolen Gardner art climbs along with it.

   _____

   _____

   _____

3. The heist took less than ten minutes—and the thieves disappeared with a four-by-six foot piece of canvas valued at more than $200 million.

   _____

   _____

   _____

Part 2: An Artist's Choices

Getting Started

Art historians often study pieces of artwork and their style. They don't think about the value of art as much. Instead, art historians think about the artist and try to answer questions about how and why he or she created the work; what places, things, or events influenced the artist; and  how a piece of art might affect history or fit into a movement of art (like Impressionism). Art critics think about what the art looks like—how beautiful it is. Critics want to give a reason for why certain pieces of art should be appreciated. Answer these questions with a partner.

1. Would you rather be an art historian or an art critic? Why?

   _____

   _____

2. What is a historical time period you have studied or are interested in? What events or places were important during that time period?

   _____

   _____

   _____

3. What current events are happening today that may influence an artist? What places or things do you find influential? What would you choose to paint?

   _____

   _____

   _____

   _____

About Unit 4: Academic Reading 2

Academic Reading 2 is from an art book published in conjunction with a special art exhibition of the artist Claude Monet (*Monet at Vétheuil: The Turning Point*). It is similar to the type of reading that would be assigned in an art history course or for someone deeply interested in the painter/artist and his/her work. This genre is similar to what you might read in other courses about the lives and work of other public figures.

Before Reading Strategy: Gauging Difficulty and Time Required

You cannot read an academic text at the same rate as you would read a newspaper or even a novel. For each type (genre) of academic text and in each discipline, you might find that you need to read things at different rates. How quickly you read will be dependent on the purpose of your reading (see page 33), including how much you need to remember. For example, think about these questions.

- Are you reading something just to get a general understanding about a topic or event?

- Are you reading material in preparation for a test?

- Are you going to have to demonstrate your understanding of the topic through class or group discussion, a presentation, or by writing a paper?

- Is the material from your textbook or from an extra, supplementary text?

How quickly you'll be able to read is also dependent on how much you already know about the topic (see page 15). The more you already know, the more quickly and efficiently you'll be able to read. However, keep in mind that even if you already know a lot about the topic <u>and</u> even if you don't have to read in preparation for a test, it doesn't mean you should only read the text once and not re-read. Your goal is still to make sure you understand the content.

In terms of determining the difficulty of a reading, there are several factors. The language, the organization, and the length all affect level of difficulty. Remember that shorter readings are not necessarily easier than longer readings.

A few other things you can do to gauge the level of difficulty and how much time you might need are listed.

1. Determine the length of the reading. Think about how much time it would take you to read a relatively easy text of this length on a topic you're familiar with or in your native language.

2. Skim the reading to see how much new or technical vocabulary is included. Factor in the time you may need to look up this new vocabulary.

3. Look at a few sentences to see how long they are. You want to get a sense of the average length of sentences in the reading. Longer sentences are usually more complex grammatically, so they may require you to re-read (more than once) to understand.

4. Look beyond the headings and special fonts (boldface or italic). What else do you notice? Does it deal with something in the past and then move forward in time to look at the future? Does it give a definition or describe something, such as a process? Does it present an argument for or against something?

5. If you think the reading is going to be difficult, mark the separate sections and subtopics so that you can read the text in pieces.

Practice Activity: Gauging Difficulty and Time Required

Find out how difficult Academic Reading 2 will be for you and how much time it will take so that you can plan your reading time. Answer the questions about each step in the process.

1. a. How long is the reading (how many pages or paragraphs)? _____

    b. How many minutes would you need to read an article of this length in your native language? _____

    c. Do you need more or less time for this reading? About how many more minutes do you need? _____

2. a. Do you know most of the words, or are there technical or new vocabulary words? _____

    b. After circling or highlighting unknown words, what percentage of them do you need to look up? _____

    c. Since important words are often repeated, how much time do you need to look those up? _____

3. a. Are there many long sentences? After reading one paragraph, what is the average sentence length?_____

    b. Are the sentences complex in grammar or detail? Can you easily identify the subjects and verbs? _____

    c. Do you need more time to focus on the topic? Will the sentence length slow your understanding? _____

    d. How much extra time should you schedule? _____

4. a. How many parts does this reading have? _____

    b. Where does each part begin? _____

    c. What does each part cover? _____

    d. Should you read the parts in one sitting, or should you break it into more than one? _____

5. Estimate the amount of time (in minutes) that you will need for this reading.

    _____

During Reading Strategy: Creating Visual and Sensory Images

Good readers purposefully create mental images as they read. Images are useful in helping readers to immerse themselves in a given time period or place, but they also help the reader engage with the material and to remember it better.

Creating visual images of what you are reading can help you focus on important details and develop a stronger overall sense of the purpose of the reading. There are many types of readings where visual and sensory imaging works, but it can be particularly useful when reading about a different period of time or about a different place. Remember that for some reading passages, it may help to think about how things might smell or feel, as well as how they might look. Be sure to think about **all of your senses** (**sight, hearing, taste, touch, smell**).

Practice Activity: Creating Visual and Sensory Images

Answer the questions.

1. Imagine life in France around 1880. What did Paris look like then? How were people dressed? How did they spend their time?

   _____

   _____

2. Paragraphs 8–10 describe a harsh winter. What senses can you use to imagine what the Seine looked like? What it felt like? What might you hear or smell?

   _____

   _____

   _____

3. The reading talks about how the death of Monet's wife Camille may have affected the way that he painted the river and depicted the scenes of winter (there was a "lonely quality" about them). Describe how something you create might be affected by loss.

   _____

   _____

   _____

Vocabulary Power

There are a number of terms and phrases in this reading that you may encounter in other academic settings. Add at least five vocabulary items to your vocabulary notebook or log.

Match the words in bold from the reading on the left with a definition on the right.

_____ 1. Claude Monet has been described by critics in this century as an **astute** observer of natural phenomena—a viewpoint summed up in the artist Cézanne's oft-quoted remark that Monet was "just an eye, but what an eye."

    a. worsened

    b. not part of

    c. aspect

_____ 2. It was during the years at Vétheuil that Monet's **nascent** technique of painting in a series was developed around the *Débâcle* paintings; sketches could be worked into more complete final form, and variants could be developed from a painting executed on site.

    d. modern

    e. growing

    f. sharp; clever

_____ 3. Some of the most startling **exclusions** include the very limited references to the presence of river traffic . . . .

    g. became

    h. happened

_____ 4. That Monet should so systematically exclude those ever-present emblems of **contemporary** commerce indicates that they were at odds with the images of that he wished to present.

_____ 5. Barge traffic is not the only **facet** of river life that is edited out of these paintings.

_____ 6. Once the Seine and other rivers in France froze over, the extreme weather conditions were **exacerbated** by a very brief thaw in late December, followed by a rapid and massive thaw on January 3, 1880.

_____ 7. . . . the accumulated snow was so deep that it brought transportation around the city and across the country almost to a halt as roads were **rendered** impassable. . . .

_____ 8. What **transpired** in Vétheuil as the surge of water and ice arrived in early January?

Academic Reading 2

Now, read the passage.

Monet's *Débâcles* Paintings

La Débâcle *by Claude Monet (1880)*

1   Claude Monet has been described by critics in this century as an astute observer of natural phenomena—a viewpoint summed up in the artist Cézanne's oft-quoted remark that Monet was "just an eye, but what an eye."[1] Monet has been considered an artist who observed and painted directly from nature. Scenes of modern life occupied him early in his career, and later he focused with greater concentration on the delicate transitions of light and color found in landscape.

2   It has been suggested that the image of Monet doing his work in the landscape was a myth that was carefully crafted by the artist himself over the years through interviews with the press, insisting that his paintings were not finished in the studio.[2] Even in his later years at Giverny, Monet perpetuated the belief that he was above all a *plein-air* painter; he was quoted by Lilla Cabot Perry as having said that he wished he had been born blind and given sight suddenly so that

1. Limello Venturi, *Impressionists and Symbolists* (New York and London, 1950): 58.
2. Although Monet indicated that the view out his window was his "studio," it may be a misinterpretation of Monet's intent to assume that he was specifically saying that he never worked indoors.

he could "see" without prior knowledge of his subject.[3] In fact, Monet did work on his paintings indoors, bringing the initial "impression" into greater finish and adjusting the chromatic and color balances within the work.[4] It was during the years at Vétheuil that Monet's nascent technique of painting in a series was developed around the *Débâcle* paintings; sketches could be worked into more complete final form, and variants could be developed from a painting executed on site. All of this fine-tuning in the studio would lead, in the fully developed series of the 1890s, to his method of ranging the related pictures of one scene around the room and adding the final touches to the ensemble.[5]

3   The traditional image of Monet as a superb observer of the natural world does not hold up under closer examination. Monet consciously selected portions of the landscape before him: in short, he edited his views of the site. Not only did he select the "view" from the sweep of the landscape before him, he also was selective as to what elements within the "view" were then included. In his paintings of the 1860s and 1870s, Monet had catered to the expectations of a leisure-based audience, including the regattas at Argenteuil.[6] This interest in fashionable recreation coincides with the depictions of these pastimes in the popular press and by other artists of his era. Yet other factors shaped Monet's "view" as well.

4   That Monet excluded certain obvious features of his environment becomes evident as the paintings are

---

3. Lilla Cabot Perry, "Reminiscences of Claude Monet from 1889–1909," *The American Magazine of Art* 18, no. 3 (March 1927): 120.

4. John House and Robert L. Herbert have discussed Monet's working methods in detail. See House, *Monet: Nature into Art* (New Haven and London, 1986) and Herbert, "Method and Meaning in Monet," *Art in America* 67 (September 1979): 90–108.

5. An interesting corollary is Monet's decision not to varnish his paintings, a change that began in the 1880s. Michael Swicklik has proposed that this allowed Monet to continue to work on his paintings, possibly years after they were begun, until he was satisfied with their state of completion. See Michael Swicklik, "French Painting and the Use of Varnish, 1750–1900," *Studies in the History of Art: Conservation Research* (Washington, 1993): 157–174.

6. Joel Isaacson, "Impressionism and Journalistic Illustration," *Arts Magazine* 56 (June, 1982): 95–115; Beatrice Farwell, *The Cult of Images*, exh. cat., The Art Museum, University of California, Santa Barbara, 1977; and Mark Roskill, "Early Impressionism and the Fashion Print," *Burlington Magazine* 112 (June 1970): 391–395.

examined for alterations and omissions. Some of the most startling exclusions include the very limited references to the presence of river traffic along the Seine, particularly barges and the tugs which directed boats along the river's shipping channels in the *Débâcle* series. Even though the Seine was one of the primary arteries for the transportation of goods through the western half of France, Monet's paintings include very few canvases in which there is any reference to this vital aspect of the river. Barge traffic on the Seine was an inescapable component of life along the river. That Monet should so systematically exclude those ever-present emblems of contemporary commerce indicates that they were at odds with the images he wished to present.

5   Barge traffic is not the only facet of river life that is edited out of these paintings. Monet excluded from his imagery all reference to the municipal passenger ferry that crossed between Vétheuil and Lavacourt. As the conduit across the river in the absence of nearby bridges over the Seine, the ferry continued to be a focus in images of both towns, as can be seen in postcards dating from the turn of the century.

6   Why would Monet so drastically alter the presentation of these towns and their relationship to the Seine? What is lost in the elimination of the barges and ferry? What is gained in the portrayal of those river scenes without commercial references? A major part of what is lost is the sense of these towns as vital participants in the life of contemporary France. Instead of bustling with economic concerns, they seem more rural than they in fact were; although the presence of human life is implied in the views of Vétheuil and Lavacourt, they rarely intrude in the landscapes. In Monet's choice of landscape motifs he prefers an English park to a corner of the forest, and the artist cannot help but put the presence of man in the landscape.

7   If the focus on contemporary French life has been deleted from these landscapes and riverscapes, what then did Monet choose to emphasize? One element that is retained is the fisherman's boat. Solitary in their pursuits, fishermen animate the stretches of water that occupy the foregrounds and middle grounds of the paintings of both towns. Did Monet in fact trade his earlier subject matter for

subjects that revisited the paintings of the preceding generation? The paintings of Argenteuil, a recreation center so easily accessible to Parisians, might have had a ready-made clientele in Paris. Monet portrayed Vétheuil and Lavacourt as agrarian hamlets removed from the *force majeur* of industrial society and modern life; there would not be an immediate audience for these paintings as souvenirs for Parisians back from holiday. The views of Vétheuil and Lavacourt, although so precisely observed as to time of day and weather, take on a timeless, elegiac aspect.

The Winter of 1879–1880 and the *Débâcles*

8   Bad weather intensified the gloom of the months following the death of Camille (the love of Monet's life) in September of 1879. Unable to paint out-of-doors, Monet undertook a series of still lifes. As winter approached, the temperature plummeted in France and the rest of Europe. The weather became a regular news feature in the periodicals and newspapers of Paris. Once the Seine and other rivers in France froze over, the extreme weather conditions were exacerbated by a very brief thaw in late December, followed by a rapid and massive thaw on January 3, 1880. The snow run-off and the cascading ice that accumulated as the Seine's thick layer of ice broke apart resulted in massive devastation. Monet, invigorated by this once-in-a-lifetime surge of large sheets of ice, created a memorable sequence of paintings to capture the river in its frozen immobility as well as its surging floods and blocks of ice.

9   The winter of 1879–1880 was one of the coldest and most severe that had been recorded in the nineteenth century; it was compared with the winters of 1870–1871 and particularly 1830–1831, when the Seine had similarly frozen.[7] The bitterest cold of the winter was experienced during the first fifteen days of December, with

---

7. The article by Georges Grison in *Le Figaro*, "La Débâcle de la Seine," lays out the history of severely cold winters in France. These hard freezes were followed by a rapid thaw and subsequent inundation. He warned that a similar devastation could result once the ice melted, but reassured readers towards the end of the article that the government was taking all possible precautions to lessen the effects of the *débâcle* when it should begin, including dynamiting the ice to facilitate the movement of chunks of ice down the Seine; see Grison, "La Débâcle de la Seine," *Le Figaro* (December 31, 1879): 2.

temperatures reaching minus 25.6 degrees C. on December 10. The snow began in earnest November 29 and continued on and off all through December; the accumulated snow was so deep that it brought transportation around the city and across the country almost to a halt as roads were rendered impassable and trains were unable to transport goods into Paris.[8] Fuel and food supplies began to run short. The river began to form a skin of ice on December 6 and within a few days had reached a thickness of ten to twelve centimeters, eventually reaching a thickness in some places of 40 or 50 centimeters, thick enough to "support veritable mountains of snow and ice."[9]

10   The breakup of the ice in the Seine at Paris, when it came, was spectacular. The thaw began on January 2, but reached its peak in the morning of January 3. Along the piers of Paris's bridges the ice accumulated with thunderous blows. Crowds thronged the quays and watched the destruction while the water rose one and a half meters between 10 am and 1 pm, and continued rising. The bridges were not the only elements of life along the river to suffer. As the water and ice surged downstream through Paris they carried away boats, barges, and other debris, breaking them apart and battering them against the piers of bridges downstream. The surge of ice and high water moved downstream to the suburbs and countryside. Throughout the country, severe flooding was observed, including extensive damage to the poplars that stood along the banks of the Marne, snapping trees that measured forty centimeters in circumference.

11   What transpired in Vétheuil as the surge of water and ice arrived in

---

8. Heavy snow fell on December 5, with enough accumulation of snow (25–30 cm) that by noon trams could not get through and circulation within Paris was impeded. "Nouvelles Diverses," *Le Figaro* (December 5, 1879): 2. Detailing the difficulty in navigating around the city, one writer for *L'Illustration* noted that pedestrians and coaches found moving nearly impossible, and omnibuses required three, four, or even five horses to pull in the snow, "Nos Gravures," *L'Illustration* 24, no. 1921 (December 20, 1879): 390.

Downriver at Vétheuil, the snowfall of early December made passage between the train station at Mantes-la-Jolie and Vétheuil impassable. When Ernest Hoschedé was returning to Vétheuil several days later, on December 8, the twelve-kilometer trip still took three hours.

9. "L'hiver a Paris," *L'Illustration* 25, no. 1923 (January 3, 1880): 7.

early January? How were Monet's immediate surroundings affected, and in what manner did Monet choose to depict the frozen Seine and the *débâcle*?

12   The paintings that Monet produced during this winter have a haunting, lonely quality that has sometimes been interpreted as continuing sorrow following the death of Camille earlier in the fall.[10] The paintings of the frozen river and *débâcle*, however, may not have indicated a mournful withdrawal. Monet may in fact simply have been responding to the extreme weather conditions. The paintings of the harsh winter at Vétheuil took the artist's winter landscapes in a new direction. Of the twenty-five works that comprise the winter paintings, very few of them include reference to human presence.[11] If Monet was to capture the continually changing, never-to-be-repeated aspects of the river as the frozen Seine became a moving mountain of ice, he may have been forced to begin a number of studies in the cold and snow which he could expand upon later in the house or at his studio space on the rue

Vintimille in Paris. Those paintings, initially begun outdoors, could then be reworked and completed away from the motif; variants could be made, or could be expanded to a larger scale.

13   Monet's paintings of the winter of 1879–1880 can be seen as an extension of the direction his painting had taken since his establishment at Vétheuil. His abandonment of the contemporary urban setting in favor of more rural, less suburban motifs can be seen again in the paintings of the frozen Seine. Throughout his career, Monet always enjoyed the challenges involved with capturing severe weather and extraordinary effects of nature. He had painted winter scenes previously, as well as rough seas along the Normandy coast. In fact, the most important painting excursion Monet undertook from Vétheuil was to the Normandy coast in 1881, where he risked life and limb in rising tides to capture certain views of the sea. It would be landscape that remained his constant subject matter henceforth.

14   The three years that Monet spent in Vétheuil proved to be a critical

---

10. See Isaacson, 1982, 5–6.
11. According to Wildenstein, 557 works contained two figures that were still visible in the painting in 1905, after which they were over-painted. See Wildenstein 1996, 2: 217.

juncture for him professionally. The acknowledged painter of contemporary life who settled in Vétheuil in 1878 departed from that town in 1881, feeling renewed and redirected. He was no longer the painter of modernity. Soon after, Monet settled farther downriver at Giverny and, through his series paintings, created a whole new understanding of landscape painting (the lilies). Many of those later innovations derived their impetus from the paintings executed of the ice-filled Seine.

After Reading Strategy: Making Connections to Other Sources

Successful academic readers are able to **make connections** between what they are reading and other sources. It very common for one academic text you are reading to make reference to other texts, graphics (pieces of art, photographs), or events and ideas. Although the writer of the text may assume readers are familiar with everything he or she references, it's unlikely that all readers will be familiar with all of the references. In these cases, what do good readers do? There are two strategies, but both involve reading the text once to get a sense of what all of the references are.

One approach is to **read the text through carefully and make a note of the references** (this does <u>not</u> mean in-text citations) **you don't know or don't understand.** You might do this by circling, underlining, or highlighting them or by making a list. Then go to a reference or online sources and begin looking for more information about each of the items on your list.

For example, in Academic Reading 2, you may not know who Cézanne was (named in the fifth line). He is described as an artist. For some readers, that may be enough information, but if it's not enough for you, then you would look up Cézanne in an encyclopedia or online to learn more about him.

After you have found more information about the people or event references that you didn't know, go back and re-read the text again. This time, you will find you have a deeper understanding of the text.

The second approach is to **skim the reading first and notice the names, places, or events that you aren't familiar with.** Again, underline, circle, or highlight them, or make a list. Then go to an encyclopedia or online and look up information about the items. Once you have that information, then begin to read the text in its entirety and refer to information you found online.

For example, in the second paragraph of Academic Reading 2, the *Débâcles* paintings are something you might want to look up so that you can refer to the paintings as you read.

Practice Activity: Making Connections to Other Sources

Check these references from Academic Reading 2 that you need to look up to make connections. Remember that what needs to be researched or understood is an individual process—your answers may not match a partner's.

_____ Lilla Cabot Perry

_____ Giverny

_____ Vétheuil

_____ the Seine

_____ the winter paintings

_____ the Marne

What other names, places, pieces of artwork, or events do you want to look up?

_____

_____

Complete the next page by writing what you know or find in a reference book or online about each item. Then draw lines between items to show connections. All items will also be connected to Monet and the _Débâcles_ paintings. A few have been done for you as examples.

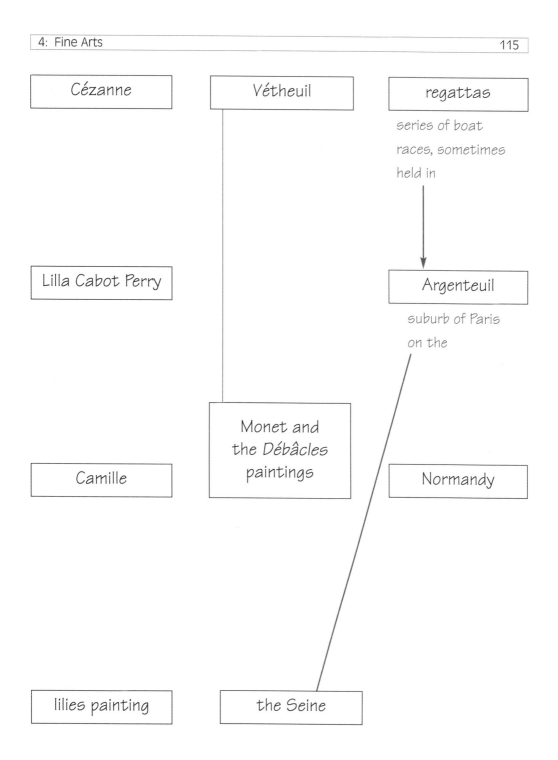

Cézanne

Vétheuil

regattas

series of boat races, sometimes held in

Lilla Cabot Perry

Argenteuil

suburb of Paris on the

Monet and the *Débâcles* paintings

Camille

Normandy

lilies painting

the Seine

Practice Activity: Reading for the Big Picture

Circle the correct information about the reading.

1. Art critics believe Monet was a *good / poor* observer of the natural world.

2. Monet working out of doors was a myth started by *the press / Monet / art critics*.

3. Monet *included / excluded* features from nature when he painted.

4. Monet emphasized *French life / the life of fishermen*.

5. Monet's pictures of frozen landscape were the result of *extreme weather / Camille's death*.

6. A critical juncture in Monet's professional life happened in *Vétheuil / Giverny*.

Summarizing What You Have Read

Summarize the main points of the original without re-using too many words or phrases from the original.

1. Scenes of modern life occupied him early in his career, and later he focused with greater concentration on the delicate transitions of light and color found in landscape.

_____

_____

_____

2. That Monet excluded certain obvious features of his environment becomes evident as the paintings are examined for alterations and omissions.

_____

_____

_____

3. The paintings that Monet produced during this winter have a haunting, lonely quality that has sometimes been interpreted as continuing sorrow following the death of Camille earlier in the fall.

_____

_____

_____

Your Active Vocabulary in the Real World

Vocabulary is important. Some words are useful for your speaking or for your writing, but other words are useful for your reading or your listening. For each word, decide how you think you will probably need this word for your English. Put a check mark (✓) under the ways you think you are likely to need the word. It is possible to have a check mark in more than one column.

YOUR VOCABULARY	I need to be able to use this word in WRITING.	I need to be able to use this word in SPEAKING.	I need to understand this word in READING.	I need to understand this word in LISTENING.
1. a ferry				
2. commodities				
3. an auction				
4. a boom				
5. severe				
6. surging				
7. on and off				
8. debris				
9. transpire				
10. tides				

Rapid Vocabulary Review

From the three answers on the right, circle the one that best explains, is an example of, or combines with the vocabulary word on the left as it is used in this unit.

Vocabulary	Answers		
Synonyms			
1. appreciation	increase	collapse	trouble
2. substantial	temporary	important	additional
3. lack	plentiful	team	missing
4. prestigious	respected	likewise	colleague
5. perpetuate	encounter	continue	reject
6. astute	perceptive	deadly	never
7. stroll	write	whisper	walk
8. pocket	illustrate	make	steal
9. pastime	fee	hobby	nation
10. exclude	omit	produce	hate
11. retain	purchase	include	keep
12. frenzy	anger	craziness	destruction
Combinations and Associations			
13. increase ___	in	with	up
14. ___ odds	at	in	on
15. prefer A ___ B	by	of	to
16. surging ___	floods	voices	windows
17. on ___ off	and	but	to
18. ___ goods	cook	friend	transport
19. proved ___ be	of	on	to
20. ___ worth	be	need	take

Vocabulary Log

To increase your vocabulary knowledge, write a definition or translation for each vocabulary item. Then write an original phrase, sentence, or note that will help you remember the vocabulary item.

Vocabulary Item	Definition or Translation	Your Original Phrase, Sentence, or Note
1. harsh	cruel, difficult	harsh winter
2. a given		
3. irrational		
4. sensible		
5. sum up		
6. estimate		
7. threaten		
8. blind		
9. variant		
10. spiral		
11. auction		
12. exuberant		
13. a subsidy		
14. boom		

Vocabulary Item	Definition or Translation	Your Original Phrase, Sentence, or Note
15. crass		
16. a sketch		
17. the turn (of the century)		
18. dips		
19. foresight		
20. drastically		
21. execute		
22. remark		
23. viewpoint		
24. motto		
25. neglect		

5 Legal Studies: Personal Law

Laws are rules that are written by institutions such as governments or schools. People may study different kinds of law in criminal justice, sociology, economics, philosophy, or history courses. Some students go to law school to become lawyers. Lawyers may argue court cases, offer legal advice, or negotiate contracts, depending on the type of law they practice. There are many different kinds of law to study: contract, criminal, property, or civil, to name a few. This unit will focus on personal law.

Part 1: Human Rights

Getting Started

Human rights are the freedoms that all people should have. Some of the rights are for the individual, but others are for the group. Some rights are legal, while others are natural. Human rights can be protected by a process called *due process*. The history of human rights is long and complicated. Answer these questions with a partner.

1. Certain characteristics, such as gender, should not deprive someone of the basic human rights. What other characteristics should not restrict a person from having the basic human rights?

   _____

   _____

   _____

   _____

2. Can you think of any basic rights, such as having access to water, that all humans should have? List them.

   _____

   _____

   _____

   _____

3. What kind of historical events may affect the violation of human rights? Are you familiar with any events in which human rights were violated?

   _____

   _____

   _____

   _____

About Unit 5: Academic Reading 1

Academic Reading 1 is from a book titled *The Ideas that Changed the World*. It is similar to what you may read in reference books and used to provide background information for topic development and research for papers and discussions. The passage discusses the history of human rights and some events that affected the definition of human rights, groups that fight for them, and the law that protects them.

Before Reading Strategy: When and How to Read Selectively

Before reading an academic passage, it is useful to think about the type of reading passage it is and think about the best way to read it to accomplish your goals.

A very important skill to develop is to know **when** and **how** to read selectively. In your academic career, you will be given many different types of reading assignments. The volume of these assignments can be overwhelming, especially when coupled with other assignments and the busy lives of today's students.

How carefully you read a text, though, depends on many factors.

- Sometimes you will not have to read a text word for word, line by line. Other times you may have to read a text several times in order to understand everything you need to understand—as when reading to prepare for a test, when reading material to use in a research paper, and when reading in your field of study.
- Good readers develop a good sense for approaching each reading assignment individually; they consider the purpose for reading, the source of the reading, and what they already know about the topic.
- Remember that just because you already know something about the topic doesn't mean you should NOT read the assignment at all. It just may mean you don't need to read it as carefully as you would other readings or allow as much time as if it were a topic you were unfamiliar with. Remember also that knowing what something is by googling it is not the same as knowing it well enough to participate in a class discussion.

- You have already learned about skimming (explicitly) and scanning (implicitly). These skills are important to read selectively. If, for instance, you need to read the text in order to find some specific pieces of information, then you might only need to **scan** to find that information. In this case, you have satisfied the requirements of the assignment. You might also not read the entire reading carefully— you might **skim**—if you are reading a lot of material to prepare to write a paper about a topic that is familiar to you and are looking for new ideas to support your own. Another reason to skim would be when you need to learn about a topic but do not need to know specific facts or details; you only need to know main ideas.
- Another reason a text might not be read in full is if you are already very familiar with the topic. In this case, you would still want to read the material, but you would be able to read it more quickly to make sure there is nothing new you need to know. For example, Academic Reading 1 comes from an encyclopedia. If your syllabus indicated that you should get some background information from a source like an encyclopedia and it was on a topic you already knew about, you would be selective in terms of what from that reading you would pay attention to. Note that it is not the case that all readings from encyclopedias should be read less carefully; this is only true if you already know something about the topic. Another example of this would be when you get assigned to read material that reviews what you already have studied or your instructor suggests other background reading.
- You might also read selectively when the material does not match your purpose. Suppose that for Academic Reading 2 in Unit 4, your instructor told you to pay attention to the biographical information about Monet because that's what you would be tested on. Since the reading includes a lot of other information besides what is relevant to Monet's life, you would be able to read this text selectively.

Practice Activity: Determining When and How to Read Selectively

Academic Reading 1 of this unit has two parts, and it has been included as an example of some background reading that might help students understand Academic Reading 2, which is a description of how the legal concept of *due process* affects our daily lives. It's possible that you may be so familiar with the concept of due process that you do not feel like you need to do the background reading. However, Academic Reading 1 is a good reading to use to practice the skill even if you already know about due process.

First, practice scanning for specific information. Scan Academic Reading 1 to find answers to these questions.

1. When did the ideas about human rights become an established concept?

   _____

2. Who and/or what is responsible for introducing the ideas about human rights?

   _____

   _____

3. What U.S. documents include the ideas about basic human rights?

   _____

4. What is the name of the most famous human rights organization?

   _____

5. Which amendment to the U.S. Constitution specifically refers to due process?

   _____

Now, practice reading selectively for the concepts only. In this case, details are not important. Read the text so that you get a sense of the main ideas.

6. List two things you learned from the text about human rights.

_____

_____

_____

_____

7. List two things you learned from the text about due process.

_____

_____

_____

_____

8. Decide how much you think you already know about due process in the United States. How much of Academic Reading 1 do you need to read? How quickly can you read it?

_____

_____

_____

_____

abc

Vocabulary Strategy: Expanding Your Vocabulary

Expanding your vocabulary is a useful strategy because it makes reading easier. The more words you know, the less you will need to stop reading to use a dictionary. As a result, your comprehension increases. This strategy is also useful for other academic tasks. For example, you can use more academic words in your discussions and your writing.

Expanding your vocabulary does not mean you have to memorize a lot of words. In Unit 3, you learned that a suffix can help you determine a word's part of speech. This knowledge is helpful because you can turn one word into several simply by changing the suffix. To expand your vocabulary further, you should be aware of roots and prefixes. While suffixes change the part of speech, prefixes and roots carry meaning.

For example, the prefix *de-* always means "away" (or "down"). The root *-tain* always means "hold" or "have." Therefore *detain* means "to hold" or "keep away or down."

My friend was *detained* because the lecture ended late.

Prefixes and roots can be mixed and matched to make many new words.

defer   desist   deduce
retain   obtain   entertain

Learn some common prefixes and roots.

Prefix	Meaning
ad-	to, toward
com-	together, with
de-	away, down
dis-	apart, not
epi-	upon
ex-	out, beyond
in-	into
inter-	between, among
mis-	wrong
mono-	alone, one
non-	not
ob-	against
over-	above

pre-	before
pro-	forward, for
re-	back, again
sub-	under
trans-	across, beyond
un-	not

Root	Meaning
-cept	take, seize
-duc, -duce, duct	lead
-fer	bear, carry
-ficient	make, do
-graph	write
-logue	say, study of
-mis, -mit	send
-plicate	fold
-pose	put, place
-scrip, -script, -scribe	write
-sist	stand
-spect	see
-ten, -tain	hold, have
-tend	stretch

In Academic Reading 1, you'll see several words using prefixes or roots (or a combination) from this list.

This modernist conception of natural laws. . . . (-cept)

. . . further advanced the concept of human rights. . . . (ad-, -cept)

. . . the UN has continued to affirm its commitment to human rights . . . . (com-, -mit)

Practice Activity: Expanding Your Vocabulary

Complete these lists.

1. What roots from the list can be used with the prefix *pro-*?

   _____

   _____

2. Which prefixes can be used with the root *-sist*?

   _____

   _____

3. What words can you create using another prefix from the list?

   _____

   _____

4. What words can you create using another root from the list?

   _____

   _____

5. List five new words using any combination of prefixes and roots from the
   lists.

   _____

   _____

Vocabulary Power

There are a number of terms and phrases in this reading that you may encounter in other academic settings. Add at least five vocabulary items to your vocabulary notebook or log.

Match the words in bold from the reading on the left with a definition on the right.

_____ 1. . . . all reflected the view that human beings are **endowed** with certain eternal and inalienable rights.

_____ 2. There are also a number of private groups involved in human rights **advocacy**.

_____ 3. . . . an organization dedicated to publicizing violations of human rights, especially freedoms of speech and religion and the right of political **dissent**.

_____ 4. Drafters of the U.S. federal Constitution adopted the due process phraseology in the Fifth Amendment, **ratified** in 1791, which provides that "No person shall . . . be deprived of life, liberty, or property, without due process of law."

_____ 5. . . . then this enactment must meet a stricter judicial **scrutiny** . . .

_____ 6. Other justices, however, have contended that states should be allowed considerable **latitude** in conducting their affairs, so long as they comply with a fundamental fairness standard.

_____ 7. Other justices, however, have contended that states should be allowed considerable latitude in conducting their affairs, so long as they **comply with** a fundamental fairness standard.

_____ 8. In determining the procedural safeguards that should be **obligatory** upon the states under the due process clause of the Fourteenth Amendment, the Supreme Court has exercised considerable supervision over the administration of criminal justice in state courts, as well as occasional influence upon state civil and administrative proceedings.

a. opposition

b. approved by vote

c. examination

d. follow the rules

e. support

f. given

g. required

h. freedom

Academic Reading 1

Now, read the passage. Many of the details (names) may not be important for this assignment.

A General Introduction to Human Rights

Human Rights

1   Human rights are the rights that belong to an individual as a consequence of being human. They refer to a wide continuum of values that are universal in character and in some sense equally claimed for all human beings.

2   The origins of the concept of human rights are usually agreed to be found in the Greco-Roman natural-law doctrines of stoicism, which held that a universal force pervades all creation and that human conduct should therefore be judged according to the law of nature, and in the *jus gentium* ("law of the nations"), in which certain universal rights were extended beyond the rights of Roman citizenship. These concepts taught more of duties than rights, however, and allowed for slavery and serfdom.*

serfdom: being in service to others

3   It was during the period from the Renaissance until the 17th century that the beliefs and practices of society so changed that the idea of human (or natural) rights could take hold as a general social need and reality. The writings of St. Thomas Aquinas and Hugo Grotius, as well as the Magna Carta, the Petition of Rights of 1628, and the English Bill of Rights, all reflected the view that human beings are endowed with certain eternal and inalienable rights.

4   This modernist conception of natural law as meaning natural rights was elaborated in the 17th and 18th centuries by such writers as René Descartes, Gottfried Leibniz, Benedict de Spinoza, and Francis Bacon. Particularly to be noted are the writings of the English philosopher John Locke, who was perhaps the most important natural-law theorist of modern times, and the Philosophes, including Denis Diderot, Voltaire, Charles-Louis de Secondat Montesquieu, and Jean-Jacques Rousseau.

5   The struggle against political absolutism in the late 18th and the 19th centuries further advanced the concept of human rights. Thomas Jefferson and the Marquis de Lafayette gave

eloquence to the plain prose of the previous century, and freedoms were specified in a variety of historic documents such as The Declaration of the Rights of Man and of the Citizen in 1789, the Bill of Rights in 1791, and the Constitution of the United States in 1787.

6   The idea that natural law is the foundation for human rights came under attack during the late 18th century by such men as conservatives Edmund Burke and David Hume, as well as by Jeremy Bentham, a founder and leading proponent of utilitarianism. This assault continued into the early 20th century. Such writers as John Stuart Mill, Friedrich Karl von Savigny, Sir Henry Maine, John Austin, and Ludwig Wittgenstein sought other justifications for, and definitions of, those rights. But efforts to assert and protect the rights of humanity continued to multiply in one form or another—the abolition of slavery, labor laws, popular education, trade unionism, universal suffrage—during the 19th and early 20th centuries, and the notion of human rights had achieved universal acceptance, at least in principle, by the second half of the 20th century, following the fall of Nazi Germany.

7   This general agreement that all human beings are entitled to some basic rights marked the birth of the international and universal recognition of human rights. In the charter establishing the United Nations, all members were pledged to achieve "universal respect for, and observance of, human rights and fundamental freedoms for all without distinction as to race, sex, language, or religion," and the UN has continued to affirm its commitment to human rights, particularly in such documents as the Universal Declaration of Human Rights in 1948.

8   International concern for human rights has also been evident outside of the United Nations. For example, the Conference on Security and Cooperation in Europe, which met in Helsinki in 1973–1975, produced the Helsinki Final Act. The European Convention for the Protection of Human Rights and Fundamental Freedoms, which first met in 1950, eventually produced the International Covenant* on Civil and Political Rights and the European Social Charter; the Ninth Pan-American Conference of 1948 adopted the American Declaration on the Rights and Duties of Man. The Organization of

covenant: agreement

African Unity in 1981 adopted the African Charter on Human and Peoples' Rights.

9   There are also a number of private groups involved in human-rights advocacy. One of the best-known international human-rights agencies is Amnesty International (founded in 1961), an organization dedicated to publicizing violations of human rights, especially freedoms of speech and religion and the right of political dissent.

Due Process

10   A course of legal proceedings according to rules and principles that have been established in a system of jurisprudence* for the enforcement and protection of private rights is known as **due process**. In each case, due process contemplates an exercise of the powers of government as the law permits and sanctions, under recognized safeguards for the protection of individual rights.

jurisprudence: the process of court decisions

11   Principally associated with one of the fundamental guarantees of the United States Constitution, due process derives from early English common law and constitutional history. The first concrete expression of the due process

idea embraced by Anglo-American law appeared in the 39th article of the Magna Carta (1215) in the royal promise that "No freeman shall be taken or (and) imprisoned . . . or exiled or in any way destroyed . . . except by the legal judgment of his peers or (and) by the law of the land." In subsequent English statutes, the references to "the legal judgment of his peers" and "laws of the land" are treated as substantially synonymous with due process of law. Drafters of the U.S. Constitution adopted the due process phraseology in the Fifth Amendment, ratified in 1791, which provides that "No person shall . . . be deprived of life, liberty, or property, without due process of law." Because this amendment was held inapplicable to state actions that might violate an individual's constitutional rights, it was not until the ratification of the Fourteenth Amendment in 1868 that several states became subject to a federally enforceable due process restraint on their legislative and procedural activities.

12   The meaning of due process as it relates to substantive enactments and procedural legislation has evolved over decades of controversial interpretation by the Supreme Court. Today, if a law

may reasonably be deemed to promote the public welfare and the means selected bear a reasonable relationship to the legitimate public interest, then the law has met the due process standard. If the law seeks to regulate a fundamental right, such as the right to travel or the right to vote, then this enactment must meet a stricter judicial scrutiny, known as the compelling interest test. Economic legislation is generally upheld if the state can point to any conceivable public benefit resulting from its enactment.

13 In determining the procedural safeguards that should be obligatory upon the states under the due process clause of the Fourteenth Amendment, the Supreme Court has exercised considerable supervision over the administration of criminal justice in state courts, as well as occasional influence upon state civil and administrative proceedings. Its decisions have been vigorously criticized, on the one hand, for unduly meddling with state judicial administration and, on the other hand, for not treating all of the specific procedural guarantees of the first 10 amendments as equally applicable to state and to federal proceedings.

14 Some justices have adhered to the proposition that the framers of the Fourteenth Amendment intended the entire Bill of Rights to be binding on the states. They have asserted that this position would provide an objective basis for reviewing state activities and would promote a desirable uniformity between state and federal rights and sanctions. Other justices, however, have contended that states should be allowed considerable latitude in conducting their affairs, so long as they comply with a fundamental fairness standard. Ultimately, the latter position substantially prevailed, and due process was recognized as embracing only those principles of justice that are "so rooted in the traditions and conscience of our people as to be ranked as fundamental." In fact, however, almost all of the Bill of Rights has by now been included among those fundamental principles.

After Reading Strategy: Using Background Reading to Prepare for More In-Depth Reading

Imagine that you have just read the background reading for a course. You know from the syllabus that you will now be asked to read several texts on the same topic that are more specific and detailed. You know that it's important to understand the background reading before continuing to the new readings.

Instructors assign background reading to provide students with the support they might need for more difficult reading assignments. Take advantage of this. **Do the background reading**—even if you only read them selectively. The important thing is to make sure you have a general understanding of the concepts and main ideas.

For example, the concepts of human rights and due process as outlined in Academic Reading 1 have been given to you because it would be very difficult to read the next reading in the unit without understanding those two concepts.

Practice Activity: Using Background Reading to Prepare for More In-Depth Reading

Analyze your understanding of the concepts of human rights and due process before you begin the second part of this unit. List what you know about these two concepts.

Human rights

_____

_____

_____

Due process

_____

_____

_____

Practice Activity: Reading for the Big Picture

Choose the best answer to each question. Write T if the statement is true or F if the statement is false.

1. _____ The idea of human rights has been a reality since Greco-Roman times.

2. _____ Human rights are common in the United States and internationally.

3. _____ Governments support human rights, but private groups are not involved.

4. _____ Due process protects the rights of governments and their laws.

5. _____ Due process has evolved over time and often in the face of controversy.

6. _____ The Bill of Rights is not yet included as fundamental principles of justice.

Summarizing What You Have Read

Summarize the main points of the original without re-using too many words or phrases from the original.

1. It was during the period from the Renaissance until the 17th century that the beliefs and practices of society so changed that the idea of human (or natural) rights could take hold as a general social need and reality.

   _____

   _____

   _____

2. A course of legal proceedings according to rules and principles that have been established in a system of jurisprudence for the enforcement and protection of private rights is known as due process.

   _____

   _____

   _____

3. The meaning of due process as it relates to substantive enactments and procedural legislation has evolved over decades of controversial interpretation by the Supreme Court.

   _____

   _____

   _____

Part 2: Due Process

Getting Started

Due process is the idea that the government has to honor or respect the rights that a person has according to the law. It protects people from harm or unfairness. Due process lets a judge in a courtroom decide what is fair rather than someone else in law enforcement. Due process is a part of the U.S. Constitution. Answer these questions with a partner.

1. Have you ever seen a legal proceeding in a court room either in real life or on a television show or in a movie? What was the case about?

   _____

   _____

   _____

   _____

2. Do you think that legal proceedings are fair? Can you think of other ways to help settle problems? List them.

   _____

   _____

   _____

   _____

3. Would you ever want to be a judge and make decisions about who is right or wrong? Why or why not?

   _____

   _____

   _____

   _____

About Unit 5: Academic Reading 2

Academic Reading 2 is from a book titled *In Our Defense: The Bill of Rights in Action* by Ellen Alderman and Caroline B. Kennedy. The book was written by two lawyers to help people understand the Bill of Rights, an important document in the United States' legal system. The book tells the true stories of people whose lives have been affected by some of the freedoms that Americans enjoy. This reading is similar to what you would read if you were using legal information as part of your research for a history or legal studies course.

Before Reading Strategy: Previewing the Type of Reading (Genre)

As a student, you will read many different types of texts, even within one course. Different "types of texts" are often referred to as **genres.** Examples of genres are letters, editorial/opinion pieces, essays, biographies, fiction, or research or other scholarly works. Each of these genres has its own set of rules for how the text is written—for example, how formal or informal it is, or what kinds of language might be common. When you know what kind of genre a text is in, it can give you a good idea what to expect before you read.

In each unit in this book, the paragraph(s) that precede the Before Reading Strategy boxes in each unit offered information about the genre of the reading to follow: *This textbook uses readings from textbooks, reference books,* etc.

This information also told you that you were going to be reading non-fiction material designed to teach or inform and that was probably written for students. For example, the information before this strategy box said that the source of Academic Reading 2 uses *true stories of people whose lives have been affected* by some of the laws and rights outlined in the U.S. Constitution.

This information is helpful in knowing what to expect about the text structure as well as the style in which it will be written—some parts will be more of a narrative and other parts might follow a cause-and-effect pattern.

However, there is more you can learn about a reading before you read that will help you. You can do this by using a couple of the other previewing strategies you have learned. The first thing you'll want to do is to skim the reading to see what you can discover about the topic and style of writing.

Practice Activity: Previewing the Type of Reading (Genre)

Answer these questions about Academic Reading 2.

1. The title of the reading includes the title of a legal case. What does that tell you about what you might expect the reading to include?

   _____

   _____

2. Review what you already know about due process. Do you think you understand it well enough to begin the reading?

   _____

   _____

3. What words or phrases related to the law and due process do you already know?

   _____

   _____

4. What are the first three words of the reading? What do they tell you about the context of the reading?

   _____

   _____

5. Read the first two sentences of the first five paragraphs. What is given in each of them? What does this tell you about how the reading is going to make its point?

   _____

   _____

During Reading Strategy: Making Text-to-Self Connections

One way that good readers engage with the text is to develop a sort of internal conversation with themselves as they read. They look for ways to make personal connections with the text and its language and concepts to help improve their understanding. They annotate the reading with these connections. Common personal connection questions readers ask or statements they think about are:

What does this remind me of?

This reminds me of . . . .

This is similar to X that I read in Y.

This looks like something I once saw in X.

This is confusing to me because of what I read/saw in X.

I agree/disagree with this because of X.

Why would this be true?

What would I do if I was in this person's [character's] situation?

I understand/don't understand why someone would do this.

Readers think about these types of things as they encounter new information, and as they continue to read, they may change their comment or question or may make new connections. Connections can also help prepare you for an exam or to write a research paper later.

Practice Activity: Making Text-to-Self Connections

As you read Academic Reading 2 on pages 144–49, stop after every paragraph, and write one note to yourself in the margin that shows how you are connecting what you are reading to your own experiences/thoughts. For example, after you read the first paragraph, make a note that indicates whether you agree with what Margarita Fuentes did and if you would or would not have done the same thing.

Vocabulary Power

There are a number of terms and phrases in this reading that you may encounter in other academic settings. Add at least five vocabulary items to your vocabulary notebook or log.

Match the words in bold from the reading on the left with a definition on the right.

_____ 1. They took the property, leaving a **bewildered** Margarita Fuentes out $400, with no stove, no stereo, and no idea what to do next.

_____ 2. Mitchell Epps of Philadelphia had **defaulted** on his payments too.

_____ 3. In addition, nothing under Pennsylvania law required that they even be told such a **remedy** was available.

_____ 4. "Nor shall any person be **deprived** of life, liberty, or property, without due process of law."

_____ 5. The due process clause in particular was intended to prevent the government from **arbitrarily** depriving persons of their most basic rights. . . .

_____ 6. Because the replevin **procedures** were authorized by state law, the suit was brought under the Fourteenth Amendment's due process clause, which restricts state action.

_____ 7. But the plaintiffs maintained that there were cases in which buyers had legitimate claims or **grievances** against a company, or were being deprived of property unfairly, or even by mistake.

_____ 8. For example, depending on the individual and governmental interests at stake, persons may be entitled to a full-blown **adversarial** proceeding in which both sides are represented by lawyers and allowed to call witnesses, while at other times, individuals may have only the right to appear before an administrative official and present their own case.

a. removed

b. confused

c. against, like enemies

d. processes

e. failed to do something

f. solution

g. complaints

h. without reason

Academic Reading 2

Now, read the passage.

Due Process of Law: *Fuentes v. Shevin*

"Nor shall any person be deprived of life, liberty, or property, without due process of law."

1   In June 1967, Margarita Fuentes of Miami bought a Firestone gas stove and service contract on an installment plan. In November, she bought a stereo. All together, she owed Firestone about $600: the stove and stereo were worth $500, and there was an extra $100 financing charge. Mrs. Fuentes made her payments for more than a year, until the stove stopped working. When she could not get anyone to come fix it, Mrs. Fuentes stopped paying. At the time, she owed $204.05. On September 15, 1969, a Firestone representative went to small claims court, filled out a form known as a writ of replevin,* and got it stamped by the court clerk. The writ of replevin authorized the sheriff to seize the stove and stereo from Mrs. Fuentes's house. It did not require that Mrs. Fuentes be notified.

2   Margarita Fuentes understood little English and spoke none. When the deputy sheriff appeared at her door later that day, she did not understand what was happening. She sent for her son-in-law, who refused to surrender the stove and stereo on the advice of his lawyer. After the sheriff explained the writ again, the son-in-law let him in, along with two men from Firestone who had been waiting outside in a truck. They took the property, leaving a bewildered Margarita Fuentes out $400, with no stove, no stereo, and no idea what to do next.

3   Pennsylvania law authorized a similar procedure. Paul and Ellen Parham purchased a Harmony House table, four stools, and a bed from Sears, Roebuck in February 1969. The property was worth $250. When Paul fell behind on the payments, Sears notified the Parhams that their account was overdue. On September 11, 1970, Sears posted a bond for double the value of the property and obtained a writ of replevin. Four days later, much to the Parhams' surprise, the sheriff arrived at their door and carted their furniture away.

What would I do?

writ of replevin: a legal solution to recover goods because they were wrongfully taken

4   Mitchell Epps of Philadelphia had defaulted on his payments, too. But he never thought he would lose his wedding ring, along with his stereo, watch, and TV roof antenna.

5   Finally, Rosa Bell Andrews Washington, a Georgia native who had recently moved to Philadelphia, was in the midst of a custody battle for her son and daughter. She had no idea how Pennsylvania law operated. But her ex-husband, Lewis Washington, was a local deputy sheriff familiar with the replevin procedure. He obtained a writ authorizing the seizure of all their son's belongings from Rosa'a house. "He had the law come in and just take stuff," says Rosa. "I was real upset." The sheriff removed the boy's bike, lamp, toys, and clothes.

6   Under Florida's law, after Firestone seized Margarita Fuentes's stove and stereo, it was obliged to sue her in court to make the repossession of the property final. Thus, she had an opportunity to challenge the removal of her property, but only after it had been taken. In Pennsylvania, there was no such procedure. If the Parhams, Epps, or Rosa Washington wanted their property back, they had to hire a lawyer and file suit themselves. In addition, nothing under Pennsylvania law required that they even be told such a remedy was available. Both Florida and Pennsylvania required that the sheriff keep repossessed property for three days, during which time individuals could get their property back if they posted a bond for double its value. After three days, it was gone for good.

7   Fuentes in Miami and Washington, Parham, and Epps in Philadelphia challenged the replevin procedure as a violation of the constitutional command that no person shall be deprived of life, liberty, or property "without due process of law." The first question was whether such everyday items were "property" covered by the Constitution at all. If they were, the next question was: What process was due? What procedure did the state have to follow before the sheriff could come and take someone's property away? The plaintiffs argued that they were at least entitled to a hearing *before* the property was repossessed.

8   Because the replevin procedures were authorized by state law, the suit was brought under the Fourteenth Amendment's due process clause, which restricts state action. The Fourteenth Amendment clause is based on the due process clause of the Fifth Amendment, which applies to the federal government. The clauses parallel each

other, with one protecting people against unfair deprivation by the states and the other by the federal government.

9   The essential purpose of the due process clause is to prevent government from acting arbitrarily. The focus is on the *procedure* itself, unlike other freedoms protected in the Bill of Rights, where the concern is with the substance and scope of the protection. The right to due process of law exists in both the criminal and civil justice systems. When "life" is at stake, procedures ensuring a fair trial and appeals process are required by due process as well as by the Sixth Amendment. "Liberty" as protected by due process has been defined to include many different interests, ranging from those of a prisoner facing actual deprivation of bodily freedom to the liberty to enter a contract, pursue a career, marry, and raise a family. The willingness of the Supreme Court to review regulations restricting these fundamental non-procedural rights has become known as substantive due process.

10   But at the time the Fifth Amendment was drafted, the focus was on pro-cedure. The origins of the due process clause can be traced back to chapter 39 of the Magna Carta, written in 1215, which provided: "No free man shall be captured or imprisoned . . . or outlawed or exiled or in any way destroyed except by the lawful judgment of his peers and by the *law of the land*."

11   The concept of providing procedural safeguards came to America with the first colonists and appears as early as 1639 in Maryland's Act for the Liberties of the People. This act essentially paraphrased the Magna Carta (using the words "laws of this province"). The first American use of the term *due process of law* was used in the amendments to the Constitution of 1787 proposed by New York State. It was then picked up by James Madison and became part of the Fifth Amendment. This simple change from "law of the land" to "due process of law" has been called a "constitutional quantum leap forward." For the words *due process* have a built-in flexibility (some argue too much flexibility) that has allowed courts to adapt the Bill of Rights to changing social conditions for more than two hundred years.

12   Nonetheless, in 1970 and 1971, district courts in both Florida and Penn-sylvania ruled against Fuentes, Epps, the Parhams, and Rosa Washington. It seemed the Constitution did not protect property on the order of a stove, a stereo, and a television antenna. The plaintiffs appealed to the U.S. Supreme Court. Their cases

were combined and became known as *Fuentes v. Shevin*. (Robert Shevin was sued in his capacity as attorney general of Florida.)

13   The plaintiffs based their Supreme Court arguments on two recently decided cases. The first, decided three years earlier, held it unconstitutional for creditors to garnish the wages of someone who owed them money (that is, have the wages paid directly to the creditors) without notice and a prior hearing. Calling the practice "most inhuman," the Court recognized that the family of someone whose wages were garnished often went hungry or without heat, and frequently the wage earner lost his or her job altogether. The second case held that the state could not cut off a person's welfare benefits without a prior hearing. To do so violated the due process clause.

14   The lawyers for Sears, Firestone, Florida, and Pennsylvania argued that the "property" at issue in those cases was far different from that in *Fuentes*. Wages and welfare benefits were "absolute necessities of life," they said; the stove and stereo were not. But the Supreme Court refused to find a constitutional difference between wages and benefits on the one hand, and consumer goods on the other. "The household goods for which the appellants contracted and paid substantial sums, are deserving of . . . protection," the Court wrote. "A stove or bed may be . . . essential to provide a minimally decent environment for human beings in their day-to-day lives. It is, after all, such consumer goods that people work and earn a livelihood in order to acquire."

15   The Court refused to get into the business of judging the relative value of the plaintiffs' selection of consumer goods. It declared, "The [due process clause] speaks of property generally. And under our free enterprise system, an individual's choices in the marketplace are respected, however unwise they may seem to someone else."

16   The states also argued that a hearing was pointless—after all, most of the plaintiffs had defaulted on their payments and admitted doing so. Holding a hearing for every person who defaulted on an installment plan would place a large and expensive burden on the state. And the end result would often be the same. The only difference would be that Sears and Firestone would repossess the property after the hearing instead of before.

17   But the plaintiffs maintained that there were cases in which buyers had legitimate claims or grievances against a company, or were being deprived of

property unfairly, or even by mistake. If buyers could prevail at a prior hearing, the inconvenience and suffering caused by the removal of their property would be avoided.

18   The Supreme Court recognized that a prior hearing would impose an additional burden and expense on the state. But it also recognized that the Bill of Rights was not written to ensure the most efficient, cost-effective system of government. It was written to protect the individual. The due process clause in particular was intended to prevent the government from arbitrarily depriving persons of their most basic rights—to life, liberty, and property—and to ensure that if such a deprivation occurred, the government be required to act according to fundamental notions of justice and fairness.

19   "The Constitution recognizes higher values than speed and efficiency," the Court explained. "Indeed, one might fairly say of the Bill of Rights in general, and the Due Process Clause in particular, that they were designed to protect the fragile values of a vulnerable citizenry from the overbearing concern for efficiency and efficacy that may characterize praiseworthy government officials." The Court did recognize that there existed emergency situations (such as wartime or danger to the public health from contaminated food) when the public interest would be so high that property could be seized without a prior hearing.

20   And the Court did not specify precisely what type of hearing would be required in the case of individuals like Fuentes. Instead, it indicated that variations in form would be acceptable in order to minimize the burden of the state. For example, depending on the individual and governmental interests at stake, persons may be entitled to a full-blown adversarial proceeding in which both sides are represented by lawyers and allowed to call witnesses, while at other times, individuals may have only the right to appear before an administrative official and present their own case. But no matter what form the hearing takes, the due process clause requires that it be a real and meaningful test, and when the individual interests are high, it must take place *before* a person can be deprived of life, liberty, or property. Some also believe that there was more to the decision than just the timing of the hearing. By coming down on the side of relatively powerless individuals against large corporate interests,

the Court was expressing its distaste for the type of economic oppression and unfair bargaining power represented by the writs of replevin.

21   By the time the Supreme Court decided *Fuentes* in June 1972, Margarita Fuentes had gotten a new stove. A highway was being built near the back of her house and she liked to cook lunch for her fellow Cubans on the road crew. This time she bought one that would hold up to heavy-duty use. The Parhams and Mitchell Epps moved on. Rosa Bell Andrews Washington lost the battle over her son, but was awarded custody of her daughter. She did not attend the Supreme Court argument and twenty years later had no idea that her case is still considered a landmark constitutional victory for ordinary Americans. Of having won, she says simply, "It feels good."

After Reading Strategy: What If You Still Don't Understand?

Sometimes even after reading and re-reading a text, good readers still don't understand as well as they should or don't understand well enough to discuss it in class or write a paper about it. What do they do? First, they don't give up on the reading, especially if the reading is in their course of study. But even if they are engineering students and the reading is on U.S. history, they don't just say, "Oh, well" and move on to their assignments for another course. Good readers develop a list of strategies for dealing with these kinds of situations. Of course, some of what they do depends on what wasn't understood.

For example, if it was the overall concept of the reading—like the concept of due process in Academic Reading 2—that you didn't understand, you would do something different than if you struggled with too much of the vocabulary.

Here are a few things you can do:

If you could understand most of the words in the reading but just weren't sure you understood the big picture concepts, like due process, you could:

- Ask someone else who does understand the concept to explain it to you. Sometimes when you aren't reading about it and can hear someone explain it, things make sense.

- Find a general reference book, like an encyclopedia, or website that will explain the concept in general terms; these entries tend to be written for people who are unfamiliar with a topic.

If you struggled with too much of the specialized or new vocabulary, you could:

- Use the vocabulary strategies you have learned in this book.

If you are not sure you understood much of the reading at all:

- Try reading the text out loud. When you read aloud, you read more slowly, which sometimes helps improve understanding. You are also hearing the information at the same time that you see it, which reinforces comprehension. Also, try pausing after each sentence to check to see if you understand what you have read so far. This allows you to focus in on the point where you stopped understanding. Once you know where you stopped understanding, you can take steps to figure out what to do next.

Practice Activity: What If You Still Don't Understand?

Answer the questions.

1. What did you not understand in Academic Reading 2? Be honest.

   _____

   _____

   _____

2. Which words or phrases were new to you?

   _____

   _____

   _____

3. What will you do to improve your level of understanding of this reading?

   _____

   _____

   _____

   _____

Practice Activity: Reading for the Big Picture

Choose the best answer to each question.

1. What is the main idea of the passage?

    a. A landmark court case gave ordinary Americans the right to their property, but not the right to life or liberty.

    b. State laws do not have to follow the laws stated in the U.S. Constitution or those of other states.

    c. A write of replevin gives ordinary Americans the right to fight state and federal laws.

    d. Ordinary Americans have the support of the Supreme Court to have their property protected.

2. Which parties won in the Supreme Court case? Choose all that are correct.

    a. Fuentes

    b. Florida

    c. Firestone

    d. Pennsylvania

    e. Rosa Bell Andrews Washington

    f. Lewis Washington

    g. Sears

    h. The Parhams

3. Why was the Supreme Court case important?

    a. It showed its support of writs of replevin.

    b. It showed its support of protection for individuals.

    c. It showed its support of burdening the state with court costs.

    d. It showed its support for saving property over life and liberty.

Summarizing What You Have Read

Write a paraphrase that expresses the main points of the original without re-using too many words or phrases from the original.

1. Because the replevin procedures were authorized by state law, the suit was brought under the Fourteenth Amendment's due process clause, which restricts state action.

   _____

   _____

   _____

2. The Fourteenth Amendment clause is based on the due process clause of the Fifth Amendment, which applies to the federal government.

   _____

   _____

   _____

3. The clauses parallel each other, with one protecting people against unfair deprivation by the states and the other by the federal government.

   _____

   _____

   _____

Your Active Vocabulary in the Real World

Vocabulary is important. Some words are useful for your speaking or for your writing, but other words are useful for your reading or your listening. For each word, decide how you think you will probably need this word for your English. Put a check mark (✓) under the ways you think you are likely to need the word. It is possible to have a check mark in more than one column.

	YOUR VOCABULARY	I need to be able to use this word in WRITING.	I need to be able to use this word in SPEAKING.	I need to understand this word in READING.	I need to understand this word in LISTENING.
1.	abolish				
2.	controversial				
3.	property				
4.	owe				
5.	refuse				
6.	so long as				
7.	bewildered				
8.	continuum				
9.	peers				
10.	due process				

Rapid Vocabulary Review

From the three answers on the right, circle the one that best explains, is an example of, or combines with the vocabulary word on the left as it is used in this unit.

Vocabulary	Answers		
Synonyms			
1. battle	fight	container	one kind of profession
2. vulnerable	ready to leave	optional	weak
3. abolish	improve	make brighter	stop; cease
4. ratify	confirm	tolerate	understand
5. controversial	people are lazy	people disagree	people need money
6. remedy	strong desire to know	a type of meeting	solution
7. refuse	connect again	provide	not accept
8. overdue	late	push; shove	poor quality
9. upset	ten items or people	upward; above	angry; bothered
10. assault	attack	enter	interfere
11. exile	ask for help	force to leave	travel in a small group
12. pledge	talk too much	promise	surrender
Combinations and Associations			
13. ___ to	deprived	custody	obliged
14. ___ burden	expensive	good	outstanding
15. be ___ deemed	reasonably	relationally	positively
16. at ___	brief	issue	new
17. on the other ___	arm	elbow	hand
18. by ___	fact	mistake	wrong
19. settle a ___	solution	population	problem
20. ___ stake	at	by	for

Vocabulary Log

To increase your vocabulary knowledge, write a definition or translation for each vocabulary item. Then write an original phrase, sentence, or note that will help you remember the vocabulary item.

Vocabulary Item	Definition or Translation	Your Original Phrase, Sentence, or Note
1. seize	to take control of	seize enemy ships
2. sought		
3. to name a few		
4. conceivable		
5. controversy		
6. charter		
7. meddle (with)		
8. custody		
9. a statute		
10. for good		
11. wages		
12. violation		
13. continuum		
14. essential		

Vocabulary Item	Definition or Translation	Your Original Phrase, Sentence, or Note
15. evident		
16. plaintiff		
17. capture		
18. elaborate		
19. file suit		
20. restrict		
21. a hearing		
22. proceeding		
23. prevail		
24. leap		
25. prose		

6 Literature: Classic Literature

Students who decide to major in English often study more than the language and its form. They also study literature. American Literature is the study of written works, such as novels, dramas, short stories, and poetry. Literature features a variety of styles and has changed throughout history. People not only study these works but read them for enjoyment. The readings in this unit are critical introductions to two well-known novels by American writers.

Part 1: *The Good Earth* by Pearl S. Buck

Getting Started

Pearl S. Buck was an American writer who was born in West Virginia, but she spent a lot of time in China because her parents were missionaries. Some of her writing is about Chinese peasants. Her novel, *The Good Earth,* was a best-selling novel in the early 1930s and won the Pulitzer Prize in 1932. She also won the Nobel Prize in Literature in 1938 and was the first American woman to win it. Answer these questions with a partner.

1. Who are your favorite writers? What did they write? Have any of them won any awards?

   _____

   _____

   _____

   _____

2. Who are some well-known American writers you are familiar with? What kind of literature do they write?

   _____

   _____

   _____

   _____

3. If you wrote a novel, what would it be about? Would it be set in your native country or in another country? Which one?

   _____

   _____

   _____

   _____

About Unit 6: Academic Reading 1

The readings in this unit are purposefully challenging and difficult so that they better replicate authentic university reading assignments.

Academic Reading 1 is a critical introduction to *The Good Earth*. A critical introduction generally appears in the pages before the beginning of a novel or at the beginning of an anthology of literature used in English courses. Critical introductions often include a brief synopsis, describe the novel's themes, and offer information about historical events at the time the novel was written and how they may have influenced the author's style and content. Often, the authors of critical introductions include information from a variety of sources. It is a good idea to read the critical introduction before reading a novel to improve comprehension and understand the author's ideas and influences. Many students make the mistake of skipping the introductory material in books or anthologies and so they miss important information about the poem, short story, or novel. One of the reasons that novels considered classic American literature (as opposed to more recent novels) include these introductions is to help students understand the importance of the novel. Even native English speakers sometimes need these critical introductions to understand the book. **Always read the introductions that appear in novels or anthologies.**

Before Reading Strategy: Previewing Other Material in Your Book

Students sometimes skip the pages at the beginning of a novel or textbook. Whether it's your textbook or another source from which you have been assigned readings, you will find material before and after the reading that might help you understand the text. For example, textbooks commonly include chronologies or other pieces of information before the units start. It's a common mistake to ignore whatever is in the textbook before the units or assigned readings.

- The **back of the book** often includes even more important information to help you as a student—an index and/or appendixes with useful information (like templates in the back of this book, Appendixes A and D). Sometimes the answer key is included in the back of book, but since many students never look at what's at the end of the book, they miss this important feature.
- There is also sometimes useful information in the **front of the book**.

The critical introduction you will read in Academic Reading 1 comes from the Simon & Schuster classic version of *The Good Earth*. In this particular edition, the publisher has included several useful additions that would help students who are not familiar with the novel or the author. One example is a chronology of Pearl Buck's life and work (for example, 1909: Buck attends boarding school in Shanghai) and a timeline explaining the historical context of *The Good Earth* for students—that is, what was happening in the world during the time of the action in the novel and the time it was published. Here are a few items from that timeline:

1882: U.S. Congress passes the Chinese Exclusion Act, which bans Chinese laborers from entering the U.S. for 10 years.

1892: The Chinese Exclusion Act is renewed for ten more years.

1911: The Qing Dynasty is overthrown, and the Republic of China is established, headed by Sun Yat-sen.

1924: U.S. Marines are sent to China to help end the civil war.

1934: The Red (Communist) Army, led by Mao Zedong, survives attacks by the Chinese Nationalist Army and undertakes the famous Long March, a journey of 6,000 miles.

1938: The Japanese seize control of Tsing-tao, Canton, and Hankow. The Chinese government retreats and sets up a new capital in Chungking.

Remember, the goal here is to understand how a timeline might help you understand the novel once you start reading. Referring to the material that is available to you as you read is a key strategy.

After the novel, the publisher included these items:

1. **Notes,** which are explanations of some of the words and phrases that may not be understood by modern readers
2. **Interpretive Notes,** which summarize the plot, the characters, and the themes and symbols in the novel. Both of these are useful to students <u>before</u> they read the book, <u>as</u> they are reading, and <u>after</u> they have read the book (to confirm understanding).

Also included in this edition are critical excerpts (information about books written about Pearl Buck and some reviews written after the book was published); questions for discussion, **which often include the types of questions an instructor might ask or that you might find on a test;** and suggestions for the interested reader, which offers some movies related to the topic of the novel and some other novels exploring the same themes.

Practice Activity: Previewing Other Material in Your Book

Answer these questions.

1. Other than the contents, what else did you find in the front of this book that might help you as a student?

    _____

    _____

2. What did you find in the back of this book that might help you with the units or the unit readings?

    _____

    _____

    _____

    _____

3. Look at a textbook for another class. Look in the back of the book (after the chapters or units). What did you find?

    _____

    _____

4. Did you find anything in the front of the book that could help you as a reader?

    _____

    _____

During Reading Strategy: Asking Questions as You Read

A helpful strategy used by good readers of academic content is **asking themselves questions as they read.** The important part of this strategy is to ask questions, not thinking about the type of questions you ask. Asking questions not only keeps you focused on the topic, but it keeps you engaged with the content. Staying engaged will better enable you to finish the reading with some level of understanding.

In academic reading, questions can help you check your level of understanding, particularly if you are reading something that is unfamiliar to you, and especially when reading fiction or about fiction.

Ask yourself important questions about the details. In fiction, ask yourself about the setting, the characters, and the time. For example, this is the first paragraph from the novel *The Good Earth:*

> It was Wang Lung's marriage day. At first, opening his eyes in the blackness of the curtains about his bed, he could not think why the dawn seemed different from any other. The house was still except for the faint, gasping cough of his old father, whose room was opposite to his own across the middle room. Every morning the old man's cough was the first sound to be heard. Wang Lung usually lay listening to it and moved only when he heard it approaching nearer and when he heard the door of his father's room squeak upon its wooden hinges.

Based only on this paragraph, the questions you might ask are:

- Do I know who all the characters are?
- Do I understand how they are related?

Practice Activity: Asking Questions as You Read

Notice the STOP signs in the margin of Reading 1. These are placed throughout the reading to remind you to stop and check your comprehension at key points. When you get to each STOP sign, stop reading and answer the questions about each section.

SECTION 1 *(page 168)*

1. Who are the main characters and what did you learn about them?

2. When and where is the story set?

SECTION 2 *(page 169)*

1. Why was *The Good Earth* an important novel in the U.S.?

SECTION 3 *(page 170)*

1. What was happening in China's history at the time the novel is set?

SECTION 4 *(page 171)*

1. What literary style is *The Good Earth?* Why?

SECTION 5 *(page 171)*

1. What is important about the author's knowledge of or experience in China?

THE END

Now that you have read the reading in its entirety, what do you think are the most important pieces of information for understanding the reading?

Vocabulary Power

There are a number of terms and phrases in this reading that you may encounter in other academic settings. Add at least five vocabulary items to your vocabulary notebook or log.

Match the words in bold from the reading on the left with a definition on the right.

_____ 1. Wang Lung's **indefatigable** spirit and O-lan's stoicism and extreme industry resonated with the American readers' belief in self-determination.

_____ 2. Wang Lung's indefatigable spirit and O-lan's **stoicism** and extreme industry resonated with the American readers' belief in self-determination.

_____ 3. Wang Lung's indefatigable spirit and O-lan's stoicism and extreme industry **resonated with** the American readers' belief in self-determination.

_____ 4. *The Good Earth* is a historically important novel because it demystified China for America and the **countless** other countries where the book appeared, either in English or in translation.

_____ 5. The resulting **treaty** gave western countries the right to station troops in China indefinitely.

_____ 6. Even if this number is greatly exaggerated, the death toll was immense during this period of **upheaval**.

_____ 7. He fears being conscripted into the army by the soldiers who are roaming the streets of the Great City; he benefits financially from the **exodus** of the wealthy with the coming of the war; and he must suffer the presence of soldiers in his own outer courtyards near the end of the novel.

_____ 8. The stories people loved best, she noted, "flowed along, clearly and simply, in the short words which they themselves used every day, with no other technique than occasional bits of description, only enough to give **vividness** to a place or a person, and never enough to delay the story. Nothing must delay the story."

a. departure

b. without end

c. a formal agreement between countries

d. was agreeable to

e. lively; colorful

f. indifference

g. disorder

h. never tired

Academic Reading 1

Now, read the passage.

The Good Earth: Demystifying the East

1   In *The Good Earth* (1931), Pearl Buck tells a timeless story about a farmer struggling to eke out a living from the earth. Hardworking and wildly ambitious, Wang Lung and his wife, O-lan, pull themselves out of poverty, bring children into the world, survive famines and floods, and toil relentlessly to build a fortune without ever losing faith in the restorative power of the land. But their work is not the novel's only story. Marriages and conniving family members, natural disasters and wars, births and adolescent rebellions and opium addiction make *The Good Earth* a rich and dramatic tapestry of life in early-twentieth-century China.

2   At the time that *The Good Earth* appeared in the United States, Chinese citizens had been barred from immigrating there for four decades, and Americans' understanding of the largest nation of the world was extremely distorted. Most Americans thought of China as a mystical place. They considered the Chinese exotic and mysterious and thought of their customs as savage and inscrutable. *The Good Earth* changed all that. Early readers of the novel recognized something familiar in it and responded enthusiastically. Wang Lung's indefatigable spirit and O-lan's

self-determinism: actions of an individual caused by the individual

stoicism and extreme industry resonated with the American readers' belief in self-determinism.* *The Good Earth* also provided early-twentieth-century readers with a framework for understanding Chinese practices that Americans viewed as peculiar. Infanticide, foot-binding, and concubinage, while still unsettling, were demystified by being presented in context.

3   While its themes are universal, *The Good Earth*'s subject, the life of a rural Chinese farmer and his wife, had been largely ignored in both English and Chinese literature at the time of its publication. Wang Lung and O-lan are unforgettable characters—sympathetic, flawed, and most important, not reducible to a stock "type." Just when we think we fully know Wang Lung and O-lan, Buck shows us yet another side of them, making them seem more real and deepening our appreciation for their humanity.

4   *The Good Earth* is a historically important novel because it demystified China for America and the countless other countries where the book appeared, either in English or in translation. But beyond its historical significance, *The Good Earth* endures because it reminds us, once again, that despite our differences—in language, culture, and religion—there are certain qualities that we share as humans. In our increasingly fractured world, this is a lesson worth remembering.

Historical and Literary Context of *The Good Earth*

China in Transition

5   *The Good Earth* is set in the early twentieth century, a tumultuous time in Chinese history. Although China had been historically closed to westerners and was suspicious of western ideas, beginning in the middle of the nineteenth century it became increasingly difficult for the country to remain immune to western influence. As a result of the Opium Wars (1839–42 and 1856–60), a series of treaties, known as the Unequal Treaties, had given western powers access to Chinese waterways and exempted western foreigners living in China from abiding by Chinese laws. Missionaries had also started streaming into the country to attempt to convert the Chinese to Christianity. Distrust of western intruders grew and culminated with the Boxer Uprising of 1889–1900, during which scores of westerners were murdered, and the United States, joined by Japan, Russia, Britain, and France, sent troops to squelch the unrest. The resulting treaty gave western countries the right to station troops in China indefinitely.

6   In 1911 the Qing dynasty, which had ruled China since the seventeenth century, was overthrown, and China descended into turmoil. For the next 38 years, until Mao Zedong proclaimed the establishment of the People's Republic of China, different political groups, including the Nationalists and the Communists, competed for dominance while outside nations, most notably Japan, fought to control different parts of the enormous country. Some historians have estimated that as many as 20 million people died in fighting immediately after the fall of the Qing dynasty. Even if this number is greatly exaggerated, the death toll was immense during this period of upheaval. To try to cement their power and wrest control from local leaders, the

Nationalist Party was forging an alliance with the small Chinese Communist Party and accepting assistance from the Soviet Union. In 1926 and 1927, the Nationalist Party launched its Northern Expedition; troops marched north, conquering local warlords along the way.

7   In the world of *The Good Earth,* Wang Lung hears rumors of a war but shows little concern for them, except when they touch his life directly. He fears being conscripted* into the army by the soldiers who are roaming the streets of the Great City; he benefits financially from the exodus of the wealthy with the coming of the war; and he must suffer the presence of soldiers in his own outer courtyards near the end of the novel. Wang Lung's view is typical of the experience of the vast majority of Chinese living in rural areas during this period. Lacking a stable central government, China was ruled *de facto* by local governments—even during the Qing dynasty. The rural population, in particular, had very little connection to the central powers. Instead, each province was ruled by local lords, to whom the rural population paid taxes. But the rural population was beginning to feel the efforts of competing groups—most notably the Nationalists and the Communists—to unite the country under one government.

conscripted:
drafted

Realism, Naturalism, and the Chinese Literary Tradition

8   Although *The Good Earth* cannot be considered a wholly American novel because Buck was bilingual and equally well versed in Chinese and English literary traditions, the novel is generally categorized as literary realism. A reaction to romanticism, realistic novels present accurate, detailed representations of ordinary people's lives. The characters are complex and three-dimensional, and their complexity stems from who they are as individuals rather than from their social positions. The plots of realistic novels are believable, their momentum driven by the choices that characters make rather than by fate or coincidence. Stylistically, realism is characterized by clarity and the use of ordinary language, giving the reader a sense of experiencing the events as the characters experience them. Other American realists include Mark Twain, whose works include *The Adventures of Tom Sawyer* (1876) and *The Adventures of Huckleberry Finn* (1885), and Henry James, author of *Daisy Miller* (1879) and *The Golden Bowl* (1904), among other books.

9   Buck often remarked that naturalism was a large influence on her work; she called her novels naturalistic. Naturalism, a literary movement, is characterized by an objective, almost scientific point of view; a focus on socioeconomic, historical, and environmental factors that determine people's fates; and an interest in the lowest classes of society. In realistic novels, the characters can overcome their backgrounds to succeed. In naturalistic novels, the characters are often crippled by factors beyond their control, pawns in whatever life their social standing dictates. While *The Good Earth* objectively renders the social and economic milieu of its protagonist,* a poor farmer, it is not a pessimistic novel. Ultimately, Buck believed too much in self-reliance and self-determinism to be a naturalist. What she might have meant when she spoke of naturalism was the openness she observed in rural China. Compared to America's Puritanism, the Chinese's frankness about such matters as birth, death, and sexual relations struck Buck as more "natural."

protagonist: main character in a novel

10   Buck's style was also influenced by the years she had spent in China. When she received the Nobel Prize in 1938, she delivered a speech entitled, "The Chinese Novel." Part of it focused on the characteristics of Chinese storytelling, a tradition that had influenced her sensibilities as a writer. The stories people loved best, she noted, "flowed along, clearly and simply, in the short words which they themselves used every day, with no other technique than occasional bits of description, only enough to give vividness to a place or a person, and never enough to delay the story. Nothing must delay the story."

After Reading Strategy: Improving Retention and Recall

As a student, you will need to develop your own strategies for **remembering what you have read and being able to recall it when needed**. It may be that you need to be able to answer questions asked by your teacher in class the next day or you may need to remember things when you write a paper or take a test. Some students make the mistake of cramming their learning into the brief period before a class or a test.

When you cram, you are not adding important information to your long-term memory. This means you will not remember everything you need to for very long. This is dangerous for students, even in subject areas that don't seem relevant to their area of study. You never know when some of the ideas you have learned in other classes will help you later in your academic study, on your job, or in life.

The annotations that you learned to make in readings will help you, as will any other notes you have. In some cases, you may simply put stars in the margin next to important ideas or events, or you may make connections to other things you have read on the same topic.

Take a minute or two after you have read an assignment to make notes in your notebook that will help you remember important items. It's not so important what you write as long it is something that will help you retain the basic information and be able to recall it when needed, such as if you are given a pop quiz.

Practice Activity: Improving Retention and Recall

Answer these questions, and then discuss them with a partner.

1. Review the two readings in Unit 4. What do you remember about each reading?

   _____

   _____

   _____

2. Review the two readings in Unit 5. What do you remember about each reading?

   _____

   _____

   _____

3. Do you think you remembered what was important from the reading? What notes would you add to this book to help you retain the information from those readings now?

_____

_____

4. Make notes in the margin or space given to help you remember this reading.

_____

_____

_____

_____

_____

_____

Practice Activity: Reading for the Big Picture

Choose the best answer to each question.

1. What is the main idea of the passage?

    a. to provide a synopsis of the story

    b. to discuss the universal themes of the novel

    c. to compare the history of the U.S. with that of China

    d. to explain how the literature was affected by history

2. Why is *The Good Earth* historically important?

    a. It was translated into many languages.

    b. It opened the relationship between China and the United States.

    c. It made China less mysterious to Americans and other nationalities.

    d. It taught readers that humans share many qualities.

Summarizing What You Have Read

Summarize the main points of the original without re-using too many words or phrases from the original.

1. At the time *The Good Earth* appeared in the United States, Chinese citizens had been barred from immigrating there for four decades, and Americans' understanding of the largest nation of the world was extremely distorted.

   _____

   _____

   _____

2. But beyond its historical significance, *The Good Earth* endures because it reminds us, once again, that despite our differences—in language, culture, and religion—there are certain qualities that we share as humans.

   _____

   _____

   _____

3. Although China had been historically closed to westerners and suspicious of western ideas, beginning in the middle of the nineteenth century it became increasingly difficult for the country to remain immune to western influence.

   _____

   _____

   _____

Part 2: *My Ántonia* by Willa Cather

Getting Started

Willa Cather was an American writer who was born in Nebraska and wrote many novels about that part of the United States. She wrote several novels, including *O Pioneers!* and *The Song of the Lark*. Her works are often required reading in English classrooms throughout the United States. It was her novel, *One of Ours*, about a young man in Nebraska during the time of World War I, that won her the Pulitzer Prize. Answer these questions with a partner.

1. What events or locations have influenced you? Would you ever write about them?

   _____

   _____

   _____

   _____

2. Cather often had a narrator tell the story of her novel. If there were a story about your life, who would you want to be the narrator? Why?

   _____

   _____

   _____

   _____

3. Imagine you were going to write a novel. Who would the main character be? Describe the character.

   _____

   _____

   _____

   _____

About Unit 6: Academic Reading 2

Academic Reading 2, like the first reading in this unit, is a critical introduction. This one is for the novel *My Ántonia* by Willa Cather.

Before Reading Strategy: Review: Which Strategies to Use?

This book has presented 11 Before Reading strategies. Good readers develop a few strategies that they will use over and over with a variety of readings. When the reading is more difficult or covers an unknown topic, good readers use other strategies that they know.

Practice Activity: Which Strategies to Use?

Review the list of Before Reading strategies presented in this book (other, more advanced strategies are presented in the other books in the series, Levels 1 and 2). Check those you feel most comfortable using or already use. Then put an X by the ones that you think might be most useful for Academic Reading 2 (see pages 180–85), which is a critical introduction to another American novel. (The lists may or may not be different.) Note that the strategies are listed in order of appearance.

____ skimming

____ determining about what you already know

____ knowing the purpose for the reading

____ preparing for a new topic

____ predicting

____ previewing text patterns

____ surveying and questioning (part of SQ3R)

____ gauging difficulty and time required

____ reading selectively

____ previewing the type of reading (genre)

____ previewing other material in the book

Which one of these will you try first? _____

Vocabulary Power

There are a number of terms and phrases in this reading that you may encounter in other academic settings. Add at least five vocabulary items to your vocabulary notebook or log.

Match the words in bold from the reading on the left with a definition on the right.

_____ 1. Her first effort, *Alexander's Bridge*, was a failure in Cather's later estimation, but this Jamesian tale of adultery set in Boston and London provided the **impetus** for three important novels . . . .

_____ 2. When Cather began working on the stories that would become the nucleus of *O Pioneers!*, writing about farmers in Nebraska amounted to a fairly severe **breach** of decorum. . . .

_____ 3. Cather was fortunate, however, that a group of iconoclastic young critics were **clamoring** for American writers to liberate themselves. . . .

_____ 4. . . . . she reproduces the national mythology of the frontier while simultaneously revising it by placing **indomitable** women at the center . . . .

_____ 5. What is probably most **distinctive** about the representation of the countryside in *My Ántonia*. . . .

_____ 6. Jim's **epiphany**, however, is very much in the American grain. . . .

_____ 7. It is important to keep in mind that Cather has created Jim as a middle-aged narrator living in New York who is looking back with **nostalgia** at his youth on the prairie.

_____ 8. Struck by Virgil's "**melancholy** reflection" that "the best days are the first to flee" (p. 159), Jim associates this sentiment of loss with his own memories of the prairie. . . .

a. remembering the past

b. unique

c. protesting, requesting

d. important realization

e. never discouraged

f. sadness

g. reason for doing something

h. violation

abc

Vocabulary Strategy: Recognizing Essential Vocabulary That Organizes Ideas

Research (see Paul Nation, *Learning Vocabulary in Another Language,* Cambridge Univeristy Press, 2001) has shown that certain words are included specifically to signal specific text patterns. This can be found in many types of academic writing—making arguments, describing how something is done, describing an event that happened, showing cause-effect relationships, and stating problems and solutions.

In some cases, these words act like pronouns that refer to another part of the text. Examples of these are words are:

assumption
case
factor
hypothesis
issue
position
question
situation

Note how they are used in these sentences:

If the supply falls, the price rises. But by how much? To answer this *question*, we must consider. . . .
Let us compare two possible *scenarios* in the oil industry: one of them relates to. . . .

In examples like these, the **function** in the sentence is often more important than the meaning of the word itself. The role of the word is to tell the reader what to expect, depending on where it is in the sentence.

Most of these words are countable abstract nouns, and they are very common in writing assignments or test prompts. For example,

Describe three *factors* that . . .
Explain the *issues* surrounding the decision to. . . .

The same research (Nation, 2001) also shows that there are three types of vocabulary that signal relationships:

1. Words that show a subordinate relationship:
   after, although, at the same time as, if, unless, so that

2. Words that connect sentences/ideas:
   in addition, also, otherwise, nevertheless, however

3. Nouns, verbs, and adjectives whose meaning is dependent on what comes before or after them in the text:
   achieve, affirm, alike, cause, compare, conclude, consequence, purpose

Practice Activity: Recognizing Essential Vocabulary That Organizes Ideas

Look for this type of vocabulary in the readings. What words can you find?

Words that refer to another part of the text (Academic Reading 1)

_____

_____

_____

Words that refer to signal relationships (Academic Reading 2)

_____

_____

_____

Academic Reading 2

Now, read the passage.

Introduction to the Novel, *My Ántonia*

1   It was not until the age of forty-five and the publication of her fourth novel, *My Ántonia* (1918), that Willa Cather established herself as a kind of poet laureate of the American prairie. Although she had been publishing poems, short fiction, and essays since the early 1890s as a precocious undergraduate at the University of Nebraska, Cather endured a long apprenticeship of spadework, first in Pittsburgh and then in New York, as a teacher, editor, and journalist. In 1912, after six frenetic years as the managing editor at *McClure's Magazine*, Cather resigned in order to launch her career as a novelist. Her first effort, *Alexander's Bridge*, was a failure in Cather's later estimation, but this Jamesian tale of adultery set in Boston and London provided the impetus for three important novels, written in quick succession, that draw heavily upon Cather's childhood on the Nebraska prairie: *O Pioneers!* (1913), *The Song of the Lark* (1915), and *My Ántonia* (1918).

2   By the time that *My Ántonia* appeared, the influential H. L. Mencken was already one of Cather's champions, but he was not alone in his superlative reaction to what he considered not only Cather's most successful novel yet, but "one of the best that any American has ever done" ("My Ántonia," p. 8; see "For Further Reading"). When Cather died in 1947, her published works included twelve novels, three collections of stories, one book of verse, a volume of essays, and a great deal of uncollected prose, much of which engages subject matter far removed in time and space from her Nebraska-inspired fiction. *Death Comes for the Archbishop* (1927), for instance, is her much-admired historical novel based on the circumstances of a nineteenth-century Catholic mission in New Mexico, while *Shadows on the Rock* (1931), set in seventeenth-century Quebec, is even more remote from the midwestern plains. Yet it is with her prairie trilogy—and *My Ántonia* in particular—that Cather defined her literary voice.

3   When Cather began working on the stories that would become the nucleus of *O Pioneers!*, writing about farmers in Nebraska amounted to a fairly severe breach of decorum, at least in the eyes of certain members of the literary establishment. Cather was fortunate, however, that a group of iconoclastic young critics were clamoring for American writers to liberate themselves from a "genteel tradition" of high culture ruled by European canons of taste and subject matter.

4   It is not surprising, then, that Cather's early novels were so well received, since their protagonists tend to fuse the qualities of the pioneer and the puritan. Set in marginal locales far from the centers of genteel culture, these works document the harsh realities of rural life and commemorate the generation of settlers who, in Cather's words, "subdued the wild land and broke up the virgin prairie" (quoted in Lee, *Willa Cather*, p. 8). Part of what makes Cather such an important voice in American literature is that she reproduces the national mythology of the frontier while simultaneously revising it by placing indomitable women at the center of the cultural script. Conquering the land,

however, is only the most obvious part of the story. What is probably most distinctive about the representation of the countryside in *My Ántonia* is the way in which Cather dwells on the more ineffable empowerment of the self as it gives itself up to an overwhelming, sublime landscape.

5   When Jim Burden, the narrator of *My Ántonia,* first arrives on the prairie, he is profoundly shaken by the featureless void into which he feels he has been marooned:

> There seemed to be nothing to see; no fences, no creeks or trees, no hills or fields. If there was a road, I could not make it out in the faint starlight. There was nothing but land: not a country at all, but the material out of which countries are made . . . I had the feeling that the world was left behind, that we had got over the edge of it, and were outside man's jurisdiction . . . If we never arrived anywhere, it did not matter. Between that earth and that sky I felt erased, blotted out. I did not say my prayers that night: here, I felt, what would be would be (p. 11).

6   In this early scene, Jim is so disoriented by an unfamiliar landscape

of absence that he feels obliterated, not uplifted, by its vastness. Like many other characters of modern literature, he is radically alone: "Outside man's jurisdiction" and beyond the power of prayer, he has been plunged into a nihilistic world where things "did not matter." Within just a few pages, however, Jim's alienation modulates into ecstasy. Captivated by the perpetual motion of the "shaggy, red grass," he realizes that the "whole country seemed, somehow, to be running" (p. 16). Rather than being terrified by the sensation that he has traversed some kind of boundary, he becomes exhilarated: "I wanted to walk straight on through the red grass and over the edge of the world, which could not be very far away" (p. 16). Finally, he gives in completely to the loss of self that is provoked by the formless landscape, within which he feels not like an individual but a mere "something":

American Transcendentalism: a movement that protested culture and society in the U.S. in the 1830s and 1840s

> I was something that lay under the
> sun and felt it, like the pumpkins,
> and I did not want to be anything
> more . . . Perhaps we feel like that
> when we die and become a part
> of something entire, whether it
> is sun and air, or goodness and

knowledge. At any rate, that is happiness; to be dissolved into something complete and great (p. 17).

Relinquishing oneself to "something complete and great" sounds more like Buddhist enlightenment than the true grit of an American pioneer. Jim's epiphany, however, is very much in the American grain, since it closely resembles what is arguably the central passage in the literature of American Transcendentalism,* in which Ralph Waldo Emerson declares, "I become a transparent eyeball; I am nothing; I see all" (*Essays and Lectures*, p. 10).

7   It is important to keep in mind that Cather has created Jim as a middle-aged narrator living in New York who is looking back with nostalgia at his youth on the prairie. In some sense, then, the epiphany in this early scene is experienced not only by a ten-year-old boy, but also by an older man coming to terms with his mortality through an act of memory. As the novel progresses, the mood becomes increasingly retrospective, since Jim becomes more and more distant from his original relationship with both the landscape and Ántonia, the companion of his youth. An important turning point in Jim's

relation to the past occurs while he is a college student studying the classics. Struck by Virgil's "melancholy reflection" that "the best days are the first to flee" (p. 159), Jim associates this sentiment of loss with his own memories of the prairie, which he finds crowding upon him during his studies. Virgil's phrase, "Optima dies...prima fugit," which is also the epigraph for *My Ántonia,* is taken from the *Georgics,* a pastoral depiction of rural life. With this reference to Virgil,* Cather places her novel in dialogue with the traditions of pastoral literature, which tend to idealize country life as simple, virtuous, and pure. Some pastoral works are also deeply elegiac, as they lament the gap between the "best days" of their legendary Arcadia* and the less noble, even corrupt present. At the point in the novel when Jim reads the classics, childhood, along with the untamed landscape of memory, become his Arcadia, a mythical spot in time to which he yearns to return. As Jim says after an emotional parting from Ántonia, "I wished I could be a little boy again, and that my way could end" (p. 192) on the prairie. Whether or not Cather shares her narrator's nostalgia has been a matter of critical debate, but there is no question that Cather asks readers to ponder how the pastoral idea of a utopian garden has affected American attitudes to the landscape and history of the nation.

8 Because the protagonists of Cather's American pastoral are primarily immigrant farmers, her work also resonates with the important and often contentious debate during the 1910s over immigration to the United States, which surged to record levels between 1880 and World War I. In the opening pages of *My Ántonia,* the reader is almost as surprised as Jim to hear a "foreign tongue" (p. 10) upon completing his journey from Virginia deep into the American heartland of Nebraska. Eventually coming into contact with a wide range of immigrants, including transplanted Bohemians (Czechs), Swedes, Norwegians, Danes, and Russians, Jim resists the xenophobia* casually expressed by his traveling companion, who believes one is "likely to get diseases from foreigners" (p. 10). This kind of animus against immigrant populations, which became prominent during the 1910s, was voiced by [people], who in

Virgil: ancient Roman poet

Arcadia: in literature, an unspoiled, harmonious wilderness

xenophobia: fear of foreigners

1920 claimed that immigrants would "in time drive us out of our own land by mere force of breeding" (quoted in Michaels, *Our America*, p. 28). Arrayed against such nativist views were figures like Randolph Bourne, who strove to remind his fellow Americans that "the Anglo-Saxon was merely the first immigrant." In his important 1916 essay "Trans-National America," Bourne even went so far as to challenge the widely accepted notion that immigrants should be completely assimilated into the "melting pot" of American society: "America is coming to be, not a nationality but a trans-nationality, a weaving back and forth, with the other lands, of many threads of all sizes and colors" (p. 262). In certain respects anticipating contemporary notions of a multicultural society, Bourne believed that the United States would be strengthened by immigrant communities that preserved their ethnic autonomy.

9   In her prairie novels, Cather echoes this conviction that immigration would enrich the nation, and this may be one reason why Bourne was so enthusiastic when he reviewed *My Ántonia*. *O Pioneers!* and *My Ántonia* are set among the immigrant farmers who struggle to cultivate the "Divide," the region near Red Cloud, Nebraska, to which Cather herself relocated with her family in 1883. In both novels, Cather favors the children of immigrants who preserve their parents' way of life. Alexandra Bergson, the Swedish heroine of *O Pioneers!*, endures lean years to become one of the most prosperous farmers in the country, but instead of Americanizing like her unappealing brothers, she holds onto Scandinavian folkways. Her home is furnished with "things her mother brought from Sweden" (*Early Novels and Stories*, p. 178), her housekeepers are Swedish girls looking to marry her Swedish farmhands, and she protects Ivar, the old Norwegian man "despised" by assimilated members of the family because, as he puts it, "I do not wear shoes, because I do not cut my hair, and because I have visions" (p. 182).

10   In some ways this persistence of the "old country" as a cultural force is even more striking in *My Ántonia*. At the end of the novel, Ántonia presides over a large family steeped in the culture of her native Bohemia. Like herself, her husband, Anton Cuzak, is a Bohemian immigrant, and since Bohemian is the language spoken at

home, their children do not learn English until they go to school. During Jim Burden's culminating visit to the Cuzak homestead, Ántonia's children boast that "Americans don't have" delicacies like their spiced plums and *kolaches* (Czech pastries), and one of her boys plays "Bohemian airs" on the violin that Ántonia's father had with him when he emigrated to Nebraska.

11   What is most interesting about this portrait of an unassimilated immigrant household is Cather's somewhat paradoxical suggestion that these kinds of families will generate an American identity still in the process of being born. In fact, Cather raises this idea that the United States remains an unformed nation in the very first chapter of the novel.

After Reading Strategy: Review: Which Strategies to Use?

This book has presented 11 After Reading strategies. Good readers develop a few strategies that they will use over and over with a variety of readings. When the reading is more difficult or on an unknown topic, good readers use other strategies that they know.

Practice Activity: Which Strategies to Use?

Review the list of After Reading strategies presented in this book (other, more advanced strategies are presented in the other books in the series, Levels 1 and 2). Check those you feel most comfortable using or already use. Then put an X by the ones that you think might be most useful to deepen your understanding of Academic Reading 2 (see pages 179–84), which is also a critical introduction to another American novel. (The lists may or may not be different.) The strategies are listed in order of appearance.

___ re-reading

___ summarizing

___ understanding details

___ deciding if the author's goals were met

___ evaluating the reading experience

___ drawing conclusions

___ reciting and reviewing (part of SQ3R)

___ making connections to other sources

___ improving retention and recall

___ using background reading to prepare for more in-depth reading

___ deciding what to do if you still don't understand

Which one will you try first?_____

Practice Activity: Reading for the Big Picture

Circle the correct information about the reading.

1. Cather's work most often drew on her *childhood in Nebraska /
    life as an editor in New York*.

2. The characters were well received because they were *pioneers /
    puritans / a combination of pioneers and puritans*.

3. Cather's characters remind people of the debate over *immigration /
    using land for farming / World War I*.

4. Cather's novels often touch on *assimilating into the melting pot /
    preserving ethnic autonomy*.

Summarizing What You Have Read

Summarize the main points of the original without re-using too many words or phrases
from the original.

1. Part of what makes Cather such an important voice in American literature is
    that she reproduces the national mythology of the frontier while simultaneously
    revising it by placing indomitable women at the center of the cultural script.

    _____

    _____

    _____

2. It is important to keep in mind that Cather has created Jim as a middle-aged
    narrator living in New York who is looking back with nostalgia at his youth
    on the prairie.

    _____

    _____

3. In certain respects anticipating contemporary notions of a multicultural
    society, Bourne believed that the United States would be strengthened by
    immigrant communities that preserved their ethnic autonomy.

    _____

    _____

    _____

Your Active Vocabulary in the Real World

Vocabulary is important. Some words are useful for your speaking or for your writing, but other words are useful for your reading or your listening. For each word, decide how you think you will probably need this word for your English. Put a check mark (✓) under the ways you think you are likely to need the word. It is possible to have a check mark in more than one column.

	YOUR VOCABULARY	I need to be able to use this word in WRITING.	I need to be able to use this word in SPEAKING.	I need to understand this word in READING.	I need to understand this word in LISTENING.
1.	revise				
2.	toil				
3.	pumpkin				
4.	adultery				
5.	conniving				
6.	share				
7.	exodus				
8.	overwhelming				
9.	indefatigable				
10.	resign				

Rapid Vocabulary Review

From the three answers on the right, circle the one that best explains, is an example of, or combines with the vocabulary word on the left as it is used in this unit.

Vocabulary	Answers		
Synonyms			
1. obliterate	destroy	upset	delete
2. enormous	very cheap	rather old	extremely big
3. ponder	small lake	think about; contemplate	travel from one country to another
4. poverty	poor	connection	dependable
5. a plot	storyline	main character	end of a story
6. a creek	largest city in an area	injury	very small stream
7. bar	aid; help	prohibit; prevent	discuss; argue
8. rural	countryside	crowded with people	unsuccessful
9. commemorate	destroy	gather	honor
10. stable	guarded	informative	unchanging; steady
11. occasional	a special event	sometimes	hidden
12. savage	keep safe; rescue	wild	plants
Combinations and Associations			
13. in the process ___	at	for	of
14. an alliance ___	up	on	with
15. stem ___	from	out	with
16. ___ point	falling	hiring	turning
17. ___ in mind	bring	keep	take
18. ___ toll	death	rumor	majority
19. the ___ of the novel	last	end	final
20. natural ___	disasters	errors	problems

Vocabulary Log

To increase your vocabulary knowledge, write a definition or translation for each vocabulary item. Then write an original phrase, sentence, or note that will help you remember the vocabulary item.

Vocabulary Item	Definition or Translation	Your Original Phrase, Sentence, or Note
1. enthusiastic	excited	The fans were enthusiastic about the team.
2. retreat		
3. tapestry		
4. despite		
5. tumultuous		
6. abide (by)		
7. adolescent		
8. enrich		
9. roam		
10. typical		
11. fate		
12. resign		
13. mystical		
14. unrest		

Vocabulary Item	Definition or Translation	Your Original Phrase, Sentence, or Note
15. contentious		
16. squelch		
17. landscape		
18. rebellion		
19. turmoil		
20. exempt		
21. prominent		
22. overcome		
23. framework		
24. upheaval		
25. coincidence		

Appendixes

Appendix A

Vocabulary Log Template

Vocabulary Item	Definition or Translation	Your Original Phrase, Sentence, or Note
1.		
2.		
3.		
4.		
5.		
6.		
7.		
8.		
9.		
10.		
11.		
12.		
13.		
14.		

Vocabulary Item	Definition or Translation	Your Original Phrase, Sentence, or Note
15.		
16.		
17.		
18.		
19.		
20.		
21.		
22.		
23.		
24.		
25.		

Appendix B

EAP Projects (Synthesizing) for Unit 1

In-Class Assignments	Outside Assignments
Paraphrase and Summarize	Mission Analysis
Look at Academic Reading 1 again. Choose one paragraph to simplify. When you are finished, compare your paraphrase with that of a partner who chose the same paragraph. Notice the things you both changed and talk about the words you changed differently. Talk about the similarities and differences. **Suggested Length:** 300 words **Preparation:** None	Find the mission statement or core purpose of a university you'd like to attend or a company you'd like to work for. You may also choose a statement of an organization or institution you belong to. Prepare a report about the mission statement and discuss how it meets the criteria of a good statement. Then discuss how the school, company, or organization maintains its core purpose while adapting its products or services. **Suggested Length:** 500 words **Preparation:** Light research in a library or online
Our Company	A Case Study
Work with a small group. Imagine you are starting a new company. Discuss what product you are selling or what service you are providing. Then write a paragraph about your company. Include details about your mission statement and core purpose as well as details about your marketing and business plans for the product(s). **Suggested Length:** 300 words **Preparation:** None	Read a case study. Research a business that you'd like to work for or are interested in. Determine a problem or a challenge the company faces (poor sales, need for more marketing, competing companies). Write a report that (1) introduces the company and its main challenge, (2) analyzes the challenge with the way the company is currently handling it, and (3) suggests a solution and/or recommendation to help the company overcome the challenge. **Suggested Length:** 800 words **Preparation:** Light research in a library or online

EAP Projects (Synthesizing) for Unit 2

In-Class Assignments	Outside Assignments
Paraphrasing and Summarizing	If The Dam Broke
Look at Academic Reading 2 again. Choose one paragraph to simplify. When you are finished, compare your paraphrase with a partner who chose the same paragraph. Notice the things you both changed and talk about the words you changed differently. Talk about the similarities and differences. **Suggested Length:** 300 words **Preparation:** None	Choose a builiding or structure from your own country or from a place you'd like to visit. Write a presentation detailing what type of structure it is, its measurements, the materials it's built from, the location, and other facts you think are interesting. Then talk about what would happen if the structure were destroyed. Include who and what would be affected. **Suggested Length:** 3–5 minutes **Preparation:** Light research in a library or online
Do the Benefits Outweigh the Drawbacks?	A Research Proposal
Integrate the material from the readings with your own ideas and thoughts. Write a short speech detailing the benefits and potential drawbacks to the Hoover Dam. Decide if you think the benefits outweigh the drawbacks and include your final decision at the end of your paragraph. **Suggested Length:** 2–3 minutes **Preparation:** None	Imagine you have been tasked with writing a research paper about a dam other than the Hoover Dam. Write a research proposal for an instructor. Include a thesis statement or research question you would focus on, why you chose the topic, two facts you would include to support your thesis or answer your question, and what sources you would use and why. **Suggested Length:** 800 words **Preparation:** Light research in a library or online

EAP Projects (Synthesizing) for Unit 3

In-Class Assignments	Outside Assignments
Cross-Cultural Comparison	**What Do You Think?**
Work with a partner who is from a culture different from yours. Choose one of the areas of proxemics described in Academic Reading 2: facial expressions, gestures, posture, or eye contact. Take notes about how your cultures are similar and different. Then write a paragraph comparing and contrasting the different cultures. Include examples. **Suggested Length:** 300 words **Preparation:** None	Do some light research, and use information from the readings to write about non-verbal communication. Decide your purpose for writing (persuade, inform), and write a short essay. Ask a partner to read your essay. Make sure the reader can tell what your purpose is. Edit as necessary before giving to your instructor. **Suggested Length:** 500 words **Preparation:** Light research in a library or online
Test Prep	**American Myths**

Imagine you have been given this topic on a test in your language class: *Describe gestures in the United States.* List any ideas you want to include. Decide on your purpose for writing (persuade, inform, etc.). Write a paragraph to address the topic as you would on a test, making it easy for your teacher to determine your purpose and logically follow your ideas. Your instructor will tell you how much time you have to write.
 	
Suggested Length: 300 words
Preparation: None
	There are some things that many people believe about the United States. Choose one of these topics to research:
	
	    fast food culture
	    gender equality in the workplace
	    rights and freedoms
	
	Do some light research to learn what people believe about the topic and whether or not it is true or a myth. Support your argument with details from your research. Choose the best organization and paraphrase or use direct quotations as needed.
	
	Suggested Length: 800 words
	Preparation: Light research in a library or online

EAP Projects (Synthesizing) for Unit 4

In-Class Assignments	Outside Assignments
Paraphrasing the Paraphrase	Art Forgery
Look at Academic Reading 2 again. Choose one paragraph to paraphrase. Write a paraphrase on a separate sheet of paper. Trade papers with a classmate and paraphrase his or her paraphrase. Continue trading papers and paraphrasing the most recent paraphrase until your instructor tells you to stop. When you receive your original paraphrase back, work with three or four classmates. See if you can identify which original paragraphs the final paraphrase goes with on their papers. Analyze the paraphrases with your group and discuss which were the best versions. **Suggested Length:** 300 words **Preparation:** None	Art forgery happens when someone creates a piece of art but claims it was done by someone else, usually a famous artist. Do some light research on the history of art forgery and on a piece of art that has been forged. Write an essay describing the history of the forged artwork and evaluate how or why you think it was forged. **Suggested Length:** 500 words **Preparation:** Light research in a library or online
For or Against Monet	Being an Art Critic
Imagine you are an art historian. Write a paragraph arguing whether or not Monet should be considered a great artist. Use information from the reading to help you support or refute your argument. **Suggested Length:** 300 words **Preparation:** None	Choose a painting by an artist you are familiar with. Write an essay that states the year the painting was created and describes the painting (its subject, colors, lines, etc.). Do some light research to determine how location or current events of the time may have influenced the artist positively or negatively. Include a picture of the piece of art. Create a short presentation to show the painting to the class and summarize your essay. **Suggested Length:** 800 words **Preparation:** Light research in a library or online

EAP Projects (Synthesizing) for Unit 5

In-Class Assignments	Outside Assignments
The History of Due Process	**A Court Case Study**
Integrate information from Academic Readings 1 and 2 to give a brief history of due process. Include only the information that you think is relevant. Cite the sources appropriately and feel free to include your own opinions about the topic. **Suggested Length:** 300 words **Preparation:** None	Work with a group and find a case that is currently awaiting trial. You can choose a case that is well-known or not. Compile your research, and evaluate the problem that prompted the court case. Then write a short essay about the case, the two sides, and a possible solution. **Suggested Length:** 500 words **Preparation:** Light research in a library or online
Types of Law	**You Be the Judge**
Many types of law are studied in law school. Imagine you want to be a lawyer. Choose one of these areas of specialty or one you are familiar with, and write a paragraph about why you would choose to be that type of lawyer. Be prepared to share your reasons with the rest of the class. Criminal lawyer Bankruptcy lawyer Corporate lawyer Discrimination lawyer Personal injury lawyer Immigration lawyer Tax lawyer **Suggested Length:** 300 words **Preparation:** None	Do some light research on a court case that you find interesting. Write an essay that describes the case and details arguments from both sides. Also include a paragraph with the judge or jury's decision, whether you agree or disagree, and reasons for your agreement or disagreement. Include citations in your essay as needed. Prepare a presentation for your classmates, but do not include the judge's decision. Lead a class discussion to see how students would judge the case. Then reveal the judge or jury's decision at the end of the discussion. **Suggested Length:** 800 words **Preparation:** Light research in a library or online

EAP Projects (Synthesizing) for Unit 6

In-Class Assignments	Outside Assignments
Buck or Cather?	You Should Read . . .
Write a paragraph about similarities Buck and Cather shared and/or differences between them. In your paragraph, explain which writer you'd most like to read novels by and why. State which parts of the critical introductions helped you make your decision and cite as needed. **Suggested Length:** 300 words **Preparation:** None	Work with a group. Choose a novelist to research, write about, and present to the class. Include details about the novelist's life, works, and influences. Prepare a written report to submit. Create a presentation to give to the class about why this novelist is one worth reading. Include visuals in your presentation if you can (perhaps pictures of the author and of historical events from the time the novelist lived and/or wrote about). **Suggested Length:** 3–5 minutes **Preparation:** Light research in a library or online
My Prompt	A Critical Introduction
Imagine you are an instructor. Write a prompt that students should be able to answer using information from Academic Reading 1 and/or Academic Reading 2. Give the prompt to your teacher and get one that another student wrote. Now imagine that you are the student. Write a response to the prompt that one of your classmates wrote. Your instructor will tell you how much time you have to write. **Suggested Length:** 300 words **Preparation:** None	Choose your favorite novel, a novel you are reading now, or a novel you are familiar with. Do some light research online or in the library to determine the author's background, the themes, and the world events that may have influenced the author. Write a critical introduction for readers who are not familiar with the author or the events happening in the world at the time the novel was written. Self-edit and peer-edit before revising your writing to submit to your instructor. **Suggested Length:** 800 words **Preparation:** Light research in a library or online

Appendix C

Common Roots and Prefixes

Continue to add to this list as you encounter new vocabulary.

Part	Meaning	Example
bene-	good	*benefit*
by-	secondary	*byproduct*
com-	together, with	*combine*
dia-	through	*diameter*
-dict-	speak	*contradict*
-dom-	home	*domestic*
-fer	carry	*transfer*
-graph-	recording	*geography, graphic*
-logue-	say, study of	*monologue*
macro-	large	*macroeconomics*
mal-	bad	*malnourished*
-mis-	send	*transmission*
multi-	many	*multimedia*
-phon-	sound	*telephone*
pre-	before	*pretest*
quad-	four	*quadrangle*
-sist-	stand	*persist*
-spect-	look	*inspect*
-struc-	build	*construction*
sub-	under	*submarine*
-ten-, -tain-	hold, have	*retain*
-tend	stretch	*extend*
-therm-	heat	*thermal*
trans-	across	*transportation*
uni-	one, single	*uniform*
-viv-	live, life	*revival*

Appendix D

Making Connections Template

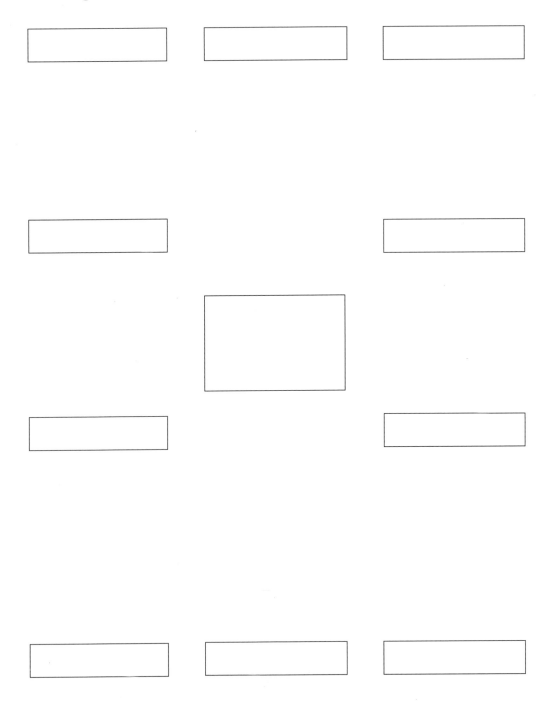